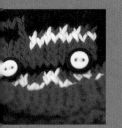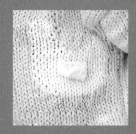

creature **comforts**
cozy knits for wee ones

amy bahrt

creature **comforts**

cozy knits for wee ones

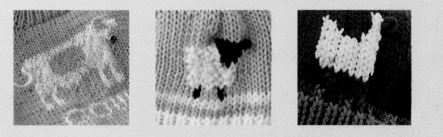

amy bahrt

❖ ❖ ❖

sixth&spring books
New York

Editorial Director
Trisha Malcolm

Art Director
Chi Ling Moy

Executive Editor
Carla Scott

Book Managers
Michelle Lo
Shannon Kerner

Instructions Editors
Charlotte Parry
Karen Greenwald

Yarn Editor
Veronica Manno

Photographer
Dan Howell

Stylist
Mary Hampton Helt

Production Managers
Lillian Esposito
David Joinnides

President, Sixth&Spring Books
Art Joinnides

233 Spring Street
New York, NY 10013

©2005 Sixth&Spring Books

Library of Congress Cataloging Control Number: 2004109336

ISBN 1-931543-66-6

Manufactured in China

1 3 5 7 9 10 8 6 4 2

First Edition, 2005

contents

❖ ❖ ❖

introduction

❖ ❖ ❖

hile I was growing up in New Jersey, I was surrounded by beautiful and whimsical antique toys, circus memorabilia, and mechanical banks, of which my parents were avid collectors. For photo opportunities, my parents would often wear enormous mouse heads, and my love of silly whimsical animals had begun. After all, how many people can claim that their parents were giant mice?

Living with two artistic parents and sister in this environment encouraged me to be creative. My first knitting experience began when I was five, when I tortured my babysitter to teach me to knit. Having no previous standard, it was very liberating to create purple acrylic scarves in wave shapes that became potholders or unusual bookmarks. Once struck with "knitted fever," my obsession continued through high school and college. When I was a student at Rhode Island School of Design, my focus was children's knitwear. Knitting for me evolved into an "art is function" form, as I found yarn to be a great canvas for creativity. With wonderful encouragement, I was able to realize my destiny: a life of yarn balls. After college, I spent over twenty years designing high-end children's sportswear and coordinating sweaters. Over the course of that time, my standard for design and color was raised.

In 1994, I started my own business of hand knits for babies. All these wonderful career experiences have helped me in putting together this book, filled with my love of offbeat colors, design and babies. Babies are the perfect audience—they instinctively respond to color, shape and movement. The designs for this book are "my babies," and I hope you will share the joy in these creations. The challenge was fitting the most creativity into the smallest amount of space!

My knits represent an old-fashioned sentiment, worked in a contemporary style. They invite interaction. Many have animal motifs: a loose ear, a kicking leg, a wiggly tail or a textured touch—something is always extending, no matter how tame it is.

To make this book more user friendly, I have kept the bodies basic. Once you start to coordinate instructions with graph numbers, your creativity with color and design will take on wings of its own. What lucky babies! Add graphs in back for a more embellished look. Novelty buttons will add uniqueness.

I hope this book serves as an inspiration to you, and allows your imagination to soar. You are bound to feel a wonderful sense of accomplishment when your baby's first words are "thanks." Start clicking and enjoy the journey!

amy bahrt

before you begin

❖ ❖ ❖

Knitting for a baby or toddlers offers myriad rewards for the knitter as well as the recipient. These smaller-scale projects can be knit over a weekend or even a day without sacrificing the long-term commitment of knitting for adults.

Moreover, knitting for children affords us the cost-effective opportunity to use up our leftover yarn stash and experiment with fun colors. There is nothing more rewarding than seeing a newborn or tot wearing a hand-stitched garment that you made with love.

Creature Comforts offers a delightful collection of knits for youngsters that is sure to inspire. With all projects knit in super-easy stockinette stitch, the basic principle behind this book is that a little color and a simple motif can transform a basic garment into an exciting work of art. Choose the silhouette, find a motif to your liking, and then select a color way—it's that easy! This principle makes for countless design options and we've formatted this book to facilitate this easy three-step design process. And with more than 60 styles in this book, we suspect that your greatest decision will be to decide which to knit first.

We encourage you to tap into your creativity and explore your color options—the results may surprise you. In addition,

details such as I-cord tails or button embellishments lend a personal touch to each design. Whether you want to knit the "Mellow Yellow" pullover or the "In the Navy" afghan or the "Tall Tales" giraffe ensemble, we're sure you'll be enchanted by the endearing designs that fill this book.

GARMENT CONSTRUCTION

Even though most of the garments in this book are made in pieces, if you are a fairly experienced knitter, you can try knitting many of them in the round, or pick up your sleeve stitches at the shoulder edge and knit down to the cuff. You just need to make some simple adjustments to the pattern.

SIZING

Since clothing measurements have changed in recent decades, it is important to measure your child to determine which size to make.

YARN SELECTION

For an exact reproduction of the projects photographed, use the yarn listed in the "Materials" section of the pattern. I've chosen yarns that are readily available in the U.S. and Canada at the time of printing. The Resources list on page 143 provides addresses of yarn distributors. Contact them for the name of a retailer in your area.

YARN SUBSTITUTION

You may wish to substitute yarns. Perhaps you view small-scale projects as a chance to incorporate leftovers from your yarn stash, or the yarn specified may not be available in your area. You'll need to knit to the given gauge to obtain the knitted measurements with a substitute yarn (see "Gauge" on page 9). Be sure to consider how the fiber content of the substitute yarn will affect the comfort and the ease of care of your projects.

After you've successfully gauge-swatched a substitute yarn, you'll need to figure out how much of the substitute yarn the project requires. First, find the total length of the original yarn in the pattern (multiply number of balls by yards/meters per ball). Divide this figure by the new yards/meters per ball (listed on the ball band). Round up to the next whole number. The answer is the number of balls required.

FOLLOWING CHARTS

Charts are a convenient way to follow colorwork, lace, cable, and other stitch patterns at a glance. These stitch charts utilize the universal knitting language of "symbolcraft." When knitting back and forth in rows, read charts from right to left on right side (RS) rows and from left to right on wrong side (WS) rows, repeating any stitch and row repeats as directed in the pattern. When knitting in the round, read charts from right to left on every round. Posting a self-adhesive note under your working row is an easy way to keep track of your place on a chart.

COLORWORK KNITTING

Two main types of colorwork are explored in this book: Intarsia and stranding.

Gauge

It is always important to knit a gauge swatch to ensure a perfect fit in a sweater. If the gauge is incorrect, a colorwork pattern may become distorted. The type of needles used—straight, circular, wood or metal—will influence gauge, so knit your swatch with the needles you plan to use for the project. Measure gauge as illustrated here. (Launder and block your gauge swatch before taking measurements). Try different needle sizes until your sample measures the required number of stitches and rows. To get fewer stitches to the inch/cm, use larger needles; to get more stitches to the inch/cm, use smaller needles. It's a good idea to keep your gauge swatch to test any embroidery or embellishment, as well as blocking and cleaning methods.

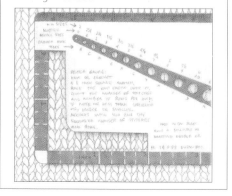

Intarsia

Intarsia is accomplished with separate bobbins of individual colors. This method is ideal for large blocks of color or for motifs that aren't repeated close together. When changing colors, always pick up the new color and wrap it around the old color to prevent holes.

Stranding

When motifs are closely placed, colorwork is accomplished by stranding along two or more colors per row, creating "floats" on the wrong side of the fabric. This technique is sometimes called Fair Isle knitting after the traditional Fair Isle patterns that are composed of small motifs with frequent color changes.

To keep an even tension and prevent holes while knitting, pick up yarns alternately over and under one another across or around. While knitting, stretch the stitches on the needle slightly wider than the length of the float at the back to keep work from puckering.

When changing colors at the beginning of rows or rounds, carry yarn along for a few rows only, or cut yarn and rejoin when needed. It is important to keep the "floats" small and neat so they don't catch when pulling on the piece.

BLOCKING

Blocking is an all-important finishing step in the knitting process. It is the best way to shape pattern pieces and smooth knitted edges in preparation for sewing together. Most garments retain their shape if the

blocking stages in the instructions are followed carefully. Choose a blocking method according to the yarn care label and when in doubt, test-block your gauge swatch.

Wet Block Method

Using rust-proof pins, pin pieces to measurements on a flat surface and lightly dampen using a spray bottle. Allow to dry before removing pins.

Steam Block Method

With WS facing, pin pieces. Steam lightly, holding the iron 2"/5cm above the knitting. Do not press or it will flatten stitches.

CARE

Refer to the yarn label for the recommended cleaning method. Many of the projects in the book can be either washed by hand, or in the machine on a gentle or wool cycle, in lukewarm water with a mild detergent. Do not agitate, or soak for more than 10 minutes. Rinse gently with tepid water, then fold in a towel and gently press the water out. Lay flat to dry away from excess heat and light. Check the yarn band for any specific care instructions such as dry cleaning or tumble drying.

DISCLAIMER

While these toys are lovely additions to any child's cache, we would also like to remind you that many of these designs require small parts, such as buttons, that can loosen or fall off. To avoid any accidents, you may want to consider embroidering faces or using alternative decorations for smaller children.

Abbreviations

approx approximately

beg begin(ning)

bind off Used to finish an edge and keep stitches from unraveling. Lift the first stitch over the second, the second over the third, etc. (UK: cast off)

cast on A foundation row of stitches placed on the needle in order to begin knitting.

cm centimeter(s)

cont continu(e)(ing)

dec decrease(ing)–Reduce the stitches in a row (knit 2 together).

foll follow(s)(ing)

g gram(s)

garter stitch Knit every row. Circular knitting: knit one round, then purl one round.

inc increase(ing)–Add stitches in a row (knit into the front and back of a stitch).

k knit

k2tog knit 2 stitches together

LH left-hand

lp(s) loop(s)

m meter(s)

M1 make one stitch–With the needle tip, lift the strand between last stitch worked and next stitch on the left-hand needle and knit into the back of it. One stitch has been added.

mm millimeter(s)

oz ounce(s)

p purl

p2tog purl 2 stitches together

pat(s) pattern

pick up and knit (purl) Knit (or purl) into the loops along an edge.

pm place markers–Place or attach a loop of contrast yarn or purchased stitch marker as indicated.

psso pass slip stitch(es) over

rem remain(s)(ing)

rep repeat

rev St st reverse stockinette stitch–Purl right-side rows, knit wrong-side rows. Circular knitting: purl all rounds. (UK: reverse stocking stitch)

rnd(s) round(s)

RH right-hand

RS right side(s)

sk skip

SKP Slip 1, knit 1, pass slip stitch over knit 1.

sl slip–An unworked stitch made by passing a stitch from the left-hand to the right-hand needle as if to purl.

ssk slip, slip, knit–Slip next 2 stitches knitwise, one at a time, to right-hand needle. Insert tip of left-hand needle into fronts of these stitches from left to right. Knit them together. One stitch has been decreased.

st(s) stitch(es)

St st Stockinette stitch–Knit right-side rows, purl wrong-side rows. Circular knitting: knit all rounds. (UK: stocking stitch)

tbl through back of loop

tog together

WS wrong side(s)

work even Continue in pattern without increasing or decreasing. (UK: work straight)

yd yard(s)

yo yarn over–Make a new stitch by wrapping the yarn over the right-hand needle. (UK: yfwd, yon, yrn)

* = Repeat directions following * as many times as indicated.

[ ] = Repeat directions inside brackets as many times as indicated.

basic cardigan & pullover

❖ ❖ ❖

Materials

- *Selected yarn*
- *One pair each sizes 5 and 7 (3.75 and 4.5mm) needles OR SIZE TO OBTAIN GAUGE*

Cardigan

- *Four buttons*

Gauge

18 sts and 24 rows to 4"/10cm over St st using larger needles.

Take time to check your gauge.

Knitted Measurements

Cardigan

- *Chest (buttoned) 23 (24, 25)"/58.5 (61, 63.5)cm*
- *Length 10½ (11, 12)"/26.5 (28, 30.5)cm*
- *Upper arm 10 (10½, 11)"/25.5 (26.5, 28)cm*

Pullover

- *Chest 23 (24, 25)"/58.5 (61, 63.5)cm*
- *Length 10½ (11, 12)"/26.5 (28, 30.5)cm*
- *Upper arm 10 (10½, 11)"/25.5 (26.5, 28)cm*

Size

6 (12, 18) months

CARDIGAN

BACK

With smaller needles and desired yarn, cast on 52 (54, 56) sts. Work in k1, p1 rib for 8 rows. Change to larger needles. Work in St st and desired pat until piece measures 10½ (11, 12)"/26.5 (28, 30.5)cm from beg. **Next row (WS)** Bind off 14 (15, 16) sts for shoulder, p24 and place on holder for neck, bind off rem 14 (15, 16) sts for shoulder.

LEFT FRONT

With smaller needles and desired yarn, cast on 24 (25, 26) sts. Work in k1, p1 rib for 8 rows. Change to larger needles. Work in St st and desired pat until piece measures 8 (8½, 9½)"/20.5 (21.5, 24)cm from beg, end with a RS row.

Neck shaping

Next row (WS) Bind off 4 sts, work to end. Cont to bind off at neck edge 2 sts twice, then 1 st twice—14 (15, 16) sts. Work even until piece measures same as back to shoulder. Bind off rem sts for shoulder.

RIGHT FRONT

Work as for left front, reversing neck shaping.

SLEEVES

With smaller needles and desired yarn, cast on 30 (30, 32) sts. Work in k1, p1 rib for 8 rows, inc 4 sts evenly across last WS row—34 (34, 36) sts. Change to larger needles. Work in St st and desired pat, AT SAME TIME, inc 1 st each side every 6th row 5 (6, 7) times—44 (46, 50) sts. Work even until piece measures 7½ (8, 9)"/19 (20.5, 23)cm from beg. Bind off all sts.

FINISHING

Sew shoulder seams. Place markers 5 (5¼, 5½)"/12.5 (13.5, 14)cm down from shoulders on front and back. Sew sleeves between markers. Sew side and sleeve seams.

Neckband

With RS facing, smaller needles and desired yarn, pick up and k 55 sts evenly around neck edge including sts on holder. Work in k1, p1 rib for 7 rows. Bind off in rib.

Buttonhole band

With RS facing, smaller needles and desired yarn, pick up and k 49 (52, 58) sts evenly along right front edge. Rib 3 rows. **Next (buttonhole) row (RS)** Rib 4 sts, [bind off 2 sts in rib, rib until there are 11 (12, 14) sts from bind-off] 3 times, bind off 2 sts in rib, rib to end. Rib next row, casting on 2 sts over bound-off sts. Rib 2 rows more. Bind off in rib.

Button band

With RS facing, smaller needles and desired yarn, pick up and k 49 (52, 58) sts evenly along left front edge. Work in k1, p1 rib for 7 rows. Bind off in rib.
Sew buttons opposite buttonholes.

PULLOVER

BACK

With smaller needles and desired yarn, cast on 52 (54, 56) sts. Work in k1, p1 rib for 8 rows. Change to larger needles. Work in St st and desired pat until piece measures 10½ (11, 12)"/26.5 (28, 30.5)cm from beg. **Next row (WS)** Bind off 14 (15, 16) sts for shoulder, p24 and place on holder for neck, bind off rem 14 (15, 16) sts for shoulder.

FRONT

Work as for back until piece measures 8 (8½, 9½)"/20.5 (21.5, 24)cm from beg.

Neck shaping

Next row (RS) K20 (21, 22) sts, join a 2nd ball of yarn and bind off center 12 sts, work to end. Working both sides at once, with separate balls of yarn, bind off 2 sts from each neck edge twice, then dec 1 st at neck edge every other row

twice. Work even until piece measures same as back to shoulders. Bind off rem 14 (15, 16) sts each side for shoulders.

SLEEVES

With smaller needles and desired yarn, cast on 30 (30, 32) sts. Work in k1, p1 rib for 8 rows, inc 4 sts evenly across last WS row—34 (34, 36) sts. Change to larger needles. Work in St st and desired pat, AT SAME TIME, inc 1 st each side every 6th row 5 (6, 7) times—44 (46, 50) sts. Work even until piece measures 7½ (8, 9)"/19 (20.5, 23)cm from beg. Bind off all sts.

FINISHING

Sew right shoulder seam.

Neckband

With RS facing, smaller needles and desired yarn, pick up and k 66 sts evenly around neck edge including sts on holder. Work in k1, p1 rib for 7 rows. Bind off in rib. Sew left shoulder and neckband seam.
Place marker 5 (5¼, 5½)"/12.5 (13.5, 14)cm down from shoulders on front and back. Sew sleeves between markers. Sew side and sleeve seams

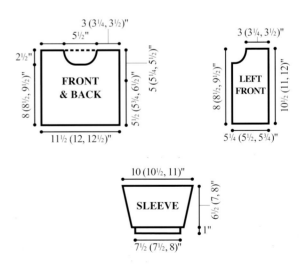

basic hat

Materials

- Selected yarn
- One pair each sizes 5 and 7 (3.75 and 4.5mm) needles OR SIZE TO OBTAIN GAUGE
- Tapestry needle

Gauge

18 sts and 24 rows to 4"/10cm over St st using larger needles.

Take time to check your gauge.

Knitted Measurements

- Head circumference 17 (18½)"/43 (47)cm

Sizes

Small/Medium (Medium/Large)

HAT

With smaller needles and desired yarn, cast on 77 (84) sts. Work in k1, p1 rib for 7 rows. Change to larger needles. Work in St st and desired pat until piece measures 4 (4½)"/10 (11.5)cm from beg.

Crown Shaping

For size Medium/Large only
Next (dec) row (RS) [K10, k2tog] 7 times—77 sts. P 1 row.

For both sizes
Next (dec) row (RS) [K9, k2tog] 7 times—70 sts. P 1 row.
Next (dec) row (RS) [K8, k2tog] 7 times—63 sts. P 1 row.
Cont in this way to dec 7 sts every RS row 5 times more—28 sts, end with a WS row.
Last (dec) row (RS) *K2tog across. Cut yarn, leaving long end. Pull yarn through rem 14 sts. Draw up tightly and sew back seam.

basic mittens & pillow

❖ ❖ ❖

Materials

- *Selected yarn*
- *One pair each sizes 7 (4.5mm) needles OR SIZE TO OBTAIN GAUGE*

Mittens

- *Tapestry needle*
- *Stitch markers*
- *Stitch holders*

Pillow

- *10"/25.5cm square pillow form*
- *Three ½"/13mm buttons*

Gauge

18 sts and 24 rows to 4"/10cm over St st using larger needles.

Take time to check your gauge.

Sizes

One size

Knitted Measurements for Pillow

10"/25.5cm square

STITCH GLOSSARY

Right increase (R-inc)
Insert RH needle into right side of the st below that on LH needle. Without twisting, slip loop onto left needle and knit.

Left increase (L-inc)
Insert LH needle into left side of the st 2 rows below stitch just knit and k through back loop.

Make one (M1)
Insert LH needle under horizontal strand between last st worked and next st on needle, K through back loop of this strand.

RIGHT MITTEN
Loosely cast on 24 sts. Work in k1, p1 rib for 7 rows. Then work in St st for 2 rows. For thumbless mitten, work even until piece measures 4½"/11.5cm from beg (or desired length). Omit thumb gusset and thumb and work top shaping.

Thumb gusset
Inc row 1 (RS) K14, pm, R-inc, k1, L-inc, pm, k to end—26 sts. P 1 row.
Inc row 2 (RS) K to marker, sl marker, R-inc, k to marker, L-inc, sl marker, k to end—28 sts. P 1 row
Rep last 2 rows once more—30 sts.

THUMB
K to marker and sl sts to holder, (remove marker), k to next marker, (remove

marker), L-inc, sl rem sts to second holder. Work even on 8 sts until thumb measures 1"/2.5cm (or desired length).
Next row (RS) K2tog across—4 sts.
Cut yarn, leaving a 16"/40.5cm tail and thread through rem sts, pull tightly to close and sew seam. With RS facing, sl sts from first holder onto needle, sl sts from second st holder onto second needle, M1, k to end—24 sts. P 1 row. Work even until piece measures 4½"/11.5cm from beg (or desired length).

Top shaping

Row 1 *K2, k2tog; rep from * to end—18 sts.
Row 2 Purl.
Row 3 *K1, k2tog; rep from * to end—12 sts.
Row 4 Purl.
Row 5 K2tog across—6 sts. Cut yarn leaving a 20"/51cm tail, pull through rem sts and draw up tightly. Sew seam.

LEFT MITTEN

Work as for right mitten to thumb gusset.

THUMB GUSSET

Inc row 1 (RS) K9, pm, R-inc, k1, L-inc, pm, k to end—26 sts. Complete as for right mitten.

PILLOW

Note: Pillow is made in one piece.
With larger needles and desired yarn, cast on 46 sts. Work in garter st for 12 rows (6 ridges), then work in St st for 33 rows, end with a RS row. K next row on WS for turning ridge. Work in St st and desired pat for 59 rows. K next row on WS for turning ridge.
Work in St st for 20 rows, then work in garter st for 6 rows (3 ridges).
Buttonhole band (RS) K10, [bind off 2 sts, work until there are 10 sts from bind-off] 3 times. K next row, casting on 2 sts over bound-off sts. Cont in garter st for 4 rows more. Bind off.

FINISHING

With RS facing, fold pillow at turning ridges, overlapping garter bands. Sew side seams working through both thicknesses of overlapped edges. Sew on buttons opposite buttonholes. Insert pillow and button closed.

pastel perfection

❖ ❖ ❖

In a sugary-sweet palette, this

fun-loving collection is designed to lend

a soft touch to your small fry's wardrobe

and nursery. The delightful motifs

are easy to knit and sure to please even

the most stylish tykes.

rush hour • cattle call • mellow yellow •
trunk show • tall tales • counting sheep

rush hour

❖ ❖ ❖

The wheels on the car go round and round all day long. Sporting this cozy hat-and-sweater set, your wee one may very well stop traffic … on the playground that is. Like the other projects, it's quick to knit in easy stockinette and boasts decorative detailing such as ribbed edges, a checkered border and sew-on buttons.

cattle call

In the <u>moooooooo</u>-d to look your best?

A lone cow with a bobble ear, chain-stitched tail

and sew-on neck bell grazes quietly on the front

of this favorable unisex pullover.

When the temperature drops, pair the sweater

with the complimentary striped watch cap.

Take a fashion cue from this youngster who

may be short in stature, but not short in taste.

This duck-motif cardigan boasts striped sleeves,

ribbed hems, and an oh-so comfy silhouette.

mellow yellow

trunk show

❖ ❖ ❖

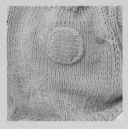

This pink little pachyderm is anything but

thick-skinned. Adorned with a knitted circle

for the ear and crochet chain for the tail,

this sweater offers maximum day-to-night

comfort. Paired with the hat,

it should wrangle plenty of compliments.

A delightful cardigan certainly garners smiles all day, but a matching pillow and baby blanket will take your wee one from playtime to naptime with ease.

tall tales

❖ ❖ ❖

counting sheep

✦ ❖ ❖

Simple stockinette stitch and minimal shaping

will have you completing these lovable

projects in two shakes of a lamb's tail! The

ribbed hat and pint-sized mittens can be knit in

a cotton-candy pink or powder blue.

rush hour

❖ ❖ ❖

Materials

Tahki Yarns/Tahki • Stacy Charles, Inc., Cotton Classic II,
1¾oz/50g skeins, each approx 74yd/68m (cotton)

- *6 skeins in #2847 blue (A)*
- *2 skeins #2712 green (B)*
- *1 skein each in #2001 white (C) and*
  #2548 yellow (D)
- *One pair each sizes 5 and 7 (3.75 and 4.5mm)*
  needles OR SIZE TO OBTAIN GAUGE
- *Stitch holder*
- *½"/13mm wheel buttons, 10 for sweater and 8*
  for hat

Sample is shown in size 18 months.

Skill level

Intermediate

BACK

Using basic pullover (page 12), cast on and work rib with B. Change to larger needles.

Beg check chart

Row 1 (RS) Work 4 sts of check chart 13 (13, 14) times, work first 0 (2, 0) sts once more. Cont as established until 4 rows of chart have been worked, then work rows 1 and 2 once more. Cont in St st with A only and complete foll basic pullover.

FRONT

Cast on and work rib with B.

Change to larger needles.

Beg check chart

Row 1 (RS) Work 4 sts of check chart 13 (13, 14) times, work first 0 (2, 0) sts once more. Cont as established until 4 rows of chart have been worked, then work rows 1 and 2 once more. Change to A and k 1 row.

check chart

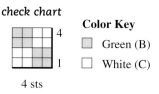

Color Key
- ▢ Green (B)
- ☐ White (C)

Beg car chart

Row 1 (WS) Work 3 (4, 5) sts A, *work 11 sts of car chart, work 6 sts A; rep from * twice more ending last rep with 4 (5, 6) sts A. Cont as established until 8 rows of chart have been worked. Cont in St st with A only and complete foll basic pullover.

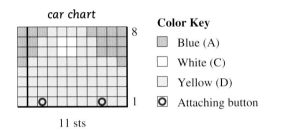

car chart

Color Key
- Blue (A)
- White (C)
- Yellow (D)
- Attaching button

8

1

11 sts

RIGHT SLEEVE

Cast on and work rib with B. Change to larger needles.

Beg check chart

Row 1 (RS) Work 4 sts of check chart 8 (8, 9) times, work first 2 (2, 0) sts once more. Cont as established until 4 rows of chart have been worked. Change to A and k 1 row,

Beg car chart

Row 1 (WS) Work 18 (18, 20) sts A, work 11 sts of car chart, work 5 sts A. Cont as established until 8 rows of chart have been worked, then work in St st with A only, AT THE SAME TIME, complete foll basic pullover.

LEFT SLEEVE

Work as for right sleeve, reversing placement of chart as foll: work 5 sts A, work 11 sts of car chart, work 18 (18, 20) sts A,

FINISHING

Complete foll basic pullover, working neckband with A.

EMBELLISHMENTS

Sew buttons to front and sleeves as indicated on chart.

HAT

Using basic hat (page 13), cast on and work rib with B. Charge to larger needles.

Beg check chart

Row 1 (RS) Work 4 sts of check chart 19 (21) times, work first 1 (0) st once more. Cont as established until 4 rows of chart have been worked. Change to A and k 1 row.

Beg car chart

Row 1 (WS) *Work 7(9) sts A, work 11 sts of car chart; rep from *, end 5 (4) sts A. Cont as established until 8 rows of chart have been worked. Cont in St st and stripe pat (9 rows A, 2 rows B, 4 rows A, 2 rows D, and 3 rows A), complete foll basic hat.

cattle call

❖ ❖ ❖

Materials

Tahki Yarns/Tahki • Stacy Charles, Inc., Cotton Classic II, 1¾oz/50g skeins, each approx 74yd/68m (cotton)

- *4 skeins in # 2837 aqua (A)*
- *2 skeins in # 2001 white (B)*
- *One pair each sizes 5 and 7 (3.75 and 4.5mm) needles OR SIZE TO OBTAIN GAUGE*
- *Crochet hook size G/6 (4mm)*
- *Stitch holder*
- *Tapestry needle*
- *Silver bell on shank ½"/13mm (may also be embroidered using silver embroidery thread)*

Sample is shown in size 12 months.

Skill level

Intermediate

STRIPE PATTERN

*2 rows B, 2 rows A; rep from * (4 rows) for stripe pat.

BACK

Using basic pullover (page 12), cast on and work rib with A. Change to larger needles. Cont in St st with A only and complete foll basic pullover.

FRONT

Cast on and work rib with A. Change to larger needles. Work in St st for 8 rows.

Beg C-O-W chart

c-o-w chart

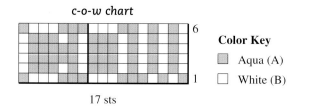

17 sts

Color Key

- ▨ Aqua (A)
- ☐ White (B)

Row 1 (RS) Work 16 (17, 18) sts A, work 17 sts of "COW" chart, work 19 (20, 21) sts A. Cont as established until 6 rows of chart have been worked. With A, work 4 rows in St st.

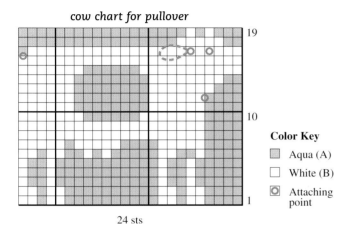

cow chart for pullover

19

10

1

24 sts

Color Key

▨ Aqua (A)
☐ White (B)
◉ Attaching point

Beg cow chart

Row 1 (RS) Work 14 (15, 16) sts A, work 24 sts of cow chart, work 14 (15, 16). Cont as established until 19 rows of chart have been worked. Cont in St st with A only and complete foll basic pullover.

SLEEVES

Cast on and work rib with A. Change to larger needles. Working in St st and stripe pat, complete foll basic pullover.

FINISHING

Complete foll basic pullover. Work neckband with A.

EMBELLISHMENTS

For eyes, use one strand of A and form French knots as indicated on chart.

For ear, with crochet hook and A, ch 8 and sew center tog. Sew as indicated on chart.

For tail, with crochet hook and B, chain 1½"/4cm. Fasten off and attach as indicated on chart.

For bell, attach as indicated on chart (optional: embroider bell using silver thread).

HAT

Using basic hat (page 13), cast on and work rib with A. Change to larger needles. Working in St st and stripe pat, complete foll basic hat.

mellow yellow

❖ ❖ ❖

Materials

Tahki Yarns/Tahki • Stacy Charles, Inc., Cotton Classic II, 1¾oz/50g skeins, each approx 74yd/68m (cotton)

- *5 skeins #2548 yellow (A)*
- *2 skeins #2001 white (B)*
- *1 skein #2712 green (C)*
- *One pair each sizes 5 and 7 (3.75 and 4.5mm) needles OR SIZE TO OBTAIN GAUGE*
- *Crochet hook size G/6 (4mm)*
- *Stitch holder*
- *Tapestry needle*
- *Four ½"/13mm white shank buttons*

Sample is shown in size 12 months.

Skill level

Intermediate

STRIPE PATTERN

*2 rows A, 2 rows B; rep from * (4 rows) for stripe pat.

BACK

Using basic cardigan (page 11), cast on and work rib with A. Change to larger needles. Work in St st with for 2 rows.

Beg check chart

Row 1 (RS) Work 6 sts of check chart 8 (9, 9) times, work first 4 (0, 2) sts once more. Cont as established until 6 rows of chart have been worked. Cont in St st with A only and complete foll basic cardigan.

LEFT FRONT

Cast on and work rib with A. Change to larger needles. Work in St st with for 2 rows.

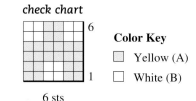

check chart

6

1

6 sts

Color Key

☐ Yellow (A)

☐ White (B)

Beg check chart

Row 1 (RS) Work 6 sts of check chart 4 times, work first 0 (1, 2) sts once more. Cont as established until 6 rows of chart have been worked. Work in St st and A for 2 rows.

Beg duck chart

Row 1 (RS) Work 4 (4, 5) sts A, work 16 sts of duck chart, work 4 (5, 5) sts A. Cont as established until 25 rows of chart have been worked. Cont in St st with A only and complete foll basic cardigan.

duck chart for cardigan

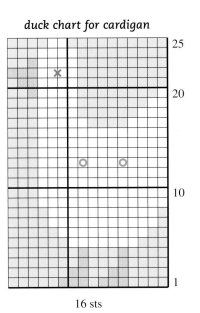

16 sts

RIGHT FRONT

Work as for left front, reversing all shaping and check chart placement and omit duck chart.

SLEEVES

Cast on and work rib with A. Change to larger needles.

Working in St st and stripe pat, complete foll basic cardigan.

Color Key
- ☐ Yellow (A)
- ☐ White (B)
- ▨ Green (C)
- ◉ Attaching point
- ☒ French knot

FINISHING

Complete foll basic cardigan. Work bands with B.

EMBELLISHMENTS

For eyes, use one strand of C and form French knots as indicated on chart.

For wing, with larger needle and B, cast on 6 sts. Work 4 rows in St st. Dec 1 st each side every other row twice. Cut yarn and draw through rem sts. Sew tightly. Attach as indicated on chart. Sew buttons to right front band opposite buttonholes.

HAT

Using basic hat (page 13), cast on and work rib with B. Change to larger needles. Work in St st for 2 rows with A.

Beg duck chart for hat

Row 1 (RS) Work 33 (36) sts A, work 11 sts of chart, work 33 (37) sts A. Cont as established until 16 rows of chart have been worked. Cont in St st with A only and complete foll basic hat.

duck chart for hat

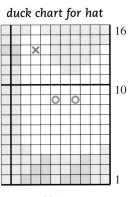

11 sts

Color Key
- ☐ Yellow (A)
- ☐ White (B)
- ▨ Green (C)
- ◉ Attaching point
- ☒ French knot

trunk show

Materials

Tahki Yarns/Tahki • Stacy Charles, Inc., Cotton Classic II, 1¾oz/50g skeins, each approx 74yd/68m (cotton)

- *5 skeins in #2712 green (A)*
- *2 skeins in #2446 pink (B)*
- *One pair each sizes 5 and 7 (3.75 and 4.5mm) needles OR SIZE TO OBTAIN GAUGE*
- *Crochet hook size G/6 (4mm)*
- *Stitch holder*
- *Tapestry needle*

Sample is shown in size 12 months.

Skill level

Intermediate

STRIPE PATTERN

*4 rows B, 4 rows A; rep from * (8 rows) for stripe pat.

BACK

Using basic pullover (page 12), cast on and work rib with A. Change to larger needles. Cont in St st with A only and complete foll basic pullover.

FRONT

Cast on and work rib with A. Change to larger needles. Work in St st for 4 rows.

Beg elephant chart

Row 1 (RS) Work 11 (12, 13) sts A, work 30 sts of elephant chart, work 11 (12, 13) sts A. Cont as established until 36 rows of chart have been worked. Cont in St st with A only and complete foll basic pullover.

elephant chart for pullover

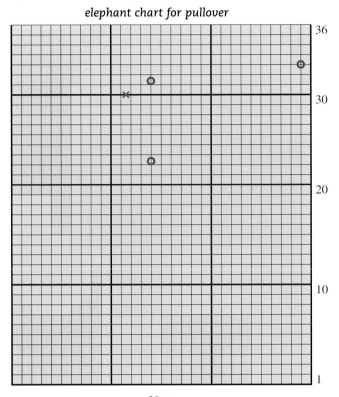

30 sts

Color Key

- ☐ Green (A)
- ☐ Pink (B)
- ◎ Attaching point
- ☒ French knot

SLEEVES

Cast on and work rib with A. Change to larger needles.

Working in St st and stripe pat, complete foll basic pullover.

FINISHING

Complete foll basic pullover. Work neckbands with A.

EMBELLISHMENTS

For eyes, use one strand of A and form French knots as indicated on chart.

For tail, with crochet hook and B, chain 2"/5cm. Fasten off and attach as indicated on chart.

For ear, with larger needles and A, cast on 6 sts. Work in St st for 2 rows. Inc 1 st each side every other row twice—10 sts. Work in St st for 4 rows more. Dec 1 st each side every other row twice—6 sts. Bind off. With A, work chain stitch around ear curve. Attach as indicated on chart.

HAT

Using basic hat (page 13), cast on and work rib with A. Change to larger needles. Working in St st and stripe pat, complete foll basic hat.

tall tales

❖ ❖ ❖

Materials

*Tahki Yarns/Tahki • Stacy Charles, Inc., Cotton Classic II,
1¾oz/50g skeins, each approx 74yd/68m (cotton)*

for cardigan

- *4 skeins in #2841 blue (A)*
- *2 skeins in #2548 yellow (B)*
- *1 skein in #2203 brown (C)*
- *One pair each sizes 5 and 7 (3.75 and 4.5mm) needles OR SIZE TO OBTAIN GAUGE*
- *Crochet hook size G/6 (4mm)*
- *Tapestry needle*
- *Four ½"/13mm blue shank buttons*

for pillow

- *5 skeins each in #2841 blue (A) and #2712 green (F)*
- *4 skeins in #2548 yellow (B)*
- *1 skein each in #2203 brown (C), #2446 pink (D) and #2001 white (E)*
- *Size 7 (4.5mm) circular needle, 32"/80cm long*
- *Crochet hook size G/6 (4mm)*
- *Stitch holder*

Sample is shown in size 12 months.

Skill level

Intermediate

GIRAFFE CARDIGAN

STRIPE PATTERN

*4 rows A, 2 rows B; rep from * (6 rows) for stripe pat.

BACK

Using basic cardigan (page 11), cast on and work rib with A. Change to larger needles work 2 rows in St st with A.

Beg block chart

Row 1 (RS) Work 4 sts of block chart 13 (13, 14) times, work first 0 (2, 0) sts once more. Cont as established until 4 rows of chart have been worked. Cont in St st with A only and complete foll basic cardigan.

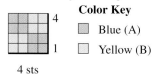

block chart for cardigan

Color Key

☐ Blue (A)
☐ Yellow (B)

4 sts

RIGHT FRONT

Cast on and work rib with A. Change to larger needles. Work 2 rows in St st with A.

Beg block chart

Row 1 (RS) Work 4 sts of block chart 6 times, work first 0 (1, 2) sts once more. Cont as established until 4 rows of chart have been worked. Work 8 rows A.

Beg giraffe chart

Row 1 (RS) Work 4 (5, 6) sts A, work 15 st of giraffe chart, work 5 sts A. Cont as established until 21 rows of chart have been worked. Cont with A only and complete foll basic cardigan.

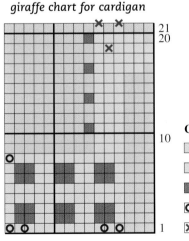

giraffe chart for cardigan

21
20

10

1

15 sts

Color Key

☐ Blue (A)
☐ Yellow (B)
■ Brown (C)
Ⓞ Attach point
☒ French knot

LEFT FRONT

Work as for right front, reversing direction and placement of chart.

SLEEVES

Cast on and work rib with B. Change to larger needles. Working in St st and stripe pat, complete foll basic cardigan.

FINISHING

Complete foll basic cardigan. Work bands with B.

EMBELLISHMENTS

For eyes use one strand of A and form French knot as indicated on chart.

For legs (make 4), with larger needles and C, cast on 5 sts. Work in garter st for 3 rows. Join B and work 9 rows in St st. Bind off. Sew wrong sides tog lengthwise and at bottom. Attach 2 legs to each giraffe as indicated on chart; leave loose.

For tail, with crochet hook and B, chain 1"/2.5cm. Fasten off and attach as indicated on chart.

For horn (knobs) with 2 strands of B, form French knot as indicated on chart.

Sew buttons to left front band opposite buttonholes.

GIRAFFE PILLOW

Cast on with A. Foll basic pillow through first turning ridge.

Cont with A and St st for 20 rows more.

Beg giraffe pillow chart

Row 1 (RS) Work 12 sts A, work 22 sts of giraffe pillow chart,

giraffe chart for pillow

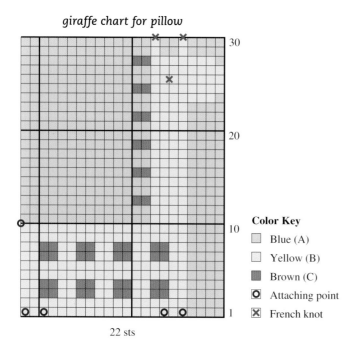

22 sts

Color Key
☐ Blue (A)
☐ Yellow (B)
☐ Brown (C)
⊙ Attaching point
☒ French knot

work 12 sts A. Cont as established until 30 rows of chart have been worked. Cont in St st with A only and work 9 rows more. Complete foll basic pillow.

FINISHING

Sew buttons opposite buttonholes.

For eye, use one strand of A and form French knots as indicated on chart.

For tail, with crochet hook and B, ch 1½"/4cm. Fasten off and attach as indicated on chart.

For horn (knobs), with 2 strands of B, form French knot as indicated on chart.

For legs (make 2), with larger needles and C, cast on 7 sts. Work in garter st for 3 rows. Join B and work 13 rows in St st. Bind off. Sew WS together lengthwise and at bottom. Attach as indicated on chart, leaving legs loose.

tall tales

❖ ❖ ❖

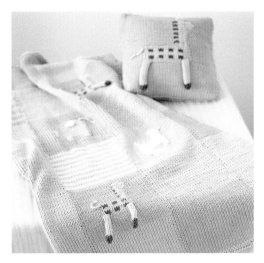

Materials

Tahki Yarns/Tahki • Stacy Charles, Inc., Cotton Classic II, 1¾oz/50g skeins, each approx 74yd/68m (cotton)

- *5 skeins each in #2841 blue (A) and #2712 green (F)*
- *4 skeins in #2548 yellow (B)*
- *1 skein each in #2203 brown (C), #2446 pink (D) and #2001 white (E)*
- *Size 7 (4.5mm) circular needle, 32"/80cm long OR SIZE TO OBTAIN GAUGE*
- *Crochet hook size G/6 (4mm)*
- *Stitch holder*

Afghan measures approx 28" x 37"/71cm x 94cm.

Skill level

Intermediate

Notes

1 Work blocks in St st with separate balls of yarn for each block. Twist yarns on WS to prevent holes.

2 4-st garter borders extend lengthwise on each side.

AFGHAN

With F, cast on 124 sts. Work in garter st for 1"/2.5cm.

Row 1 (RS) Cont 4 sts garter st with F, work blocks in St st, foll diagram for placement, cont last 4 sts in garter st with F. Cont as established until all blocks have been worked. With F, work in garter st for 1"/2.5cm. Bind off.

SOLID BLOCK

Cast on 29 sts and work 36 rows with A, B and F.

STRIPE BLOCK 1

Cast on 29 sts as work 36 rows as foll: [4 rows D, 4 rows F] 4 times, 4 rows D.

STRIPE BLOCK 2

Cast on 29 sts as work 36 rows as foll:

[2 rows B, 2 rows E] 9 times.

STRIPE BLOCK 3

Cast on 29 sts as work 36 rows as foll:

[4 rows A, 2 rows B] 6 times.

GIRAFFE BLOCK

29 sts and 36 rows as foll:

Rows 1 to 12 St st with A.

Rows 13 to 33 Work 21 rows of giraffe chart as foll: 7 sts A, 15 sts giraffe chart, 7 sts A.

Rows 34 to 36 St st with A.

DUCK BLOCK

29 sts and 36 rows as foll:

Rows 1 to 6 St st with B.

Rows 7 to 31 Work 25 rows of duck chart as foll: 6 sts B, 16 sts duck chart, 7 sts B.

Rows 32 to 36 St st with B.

giraffe chart

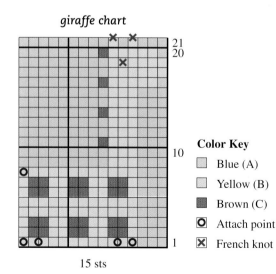

Color Key

▢	Blue (A)
▢	Yellow (B)
◼	Brown (C)
Ⓞ	Attach point
☒	French knot

15 sts

duck chart

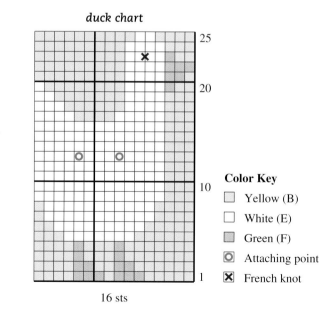

Color Key

▢	Yellow (B)
▢	White (E)
▨	Green (F)
Ⓞ	Attaching point
☒	French knot

16 sts

elephant chart

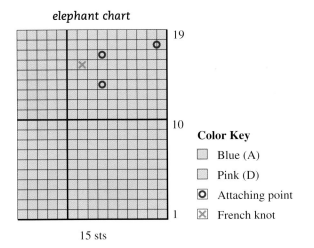

19

10

1

15 sts

Color Key

☐ Blue (A)

☐ Pink (D)

◉ Attaching point

☒ French knot

ELEPHANT BLOCK

29 sts and 36 rows as foll:

Rows 1 to 8 St st with A.

Rows 9 to 27 Work 19 rows of elephant chart as foll: 7 sts A,

15 sts elephant chart, 7 sts A.

Rows 28 to 36 St st with A.

FINISHING

Giraffe: See instructions for finishing chart for giraffe cardigan.

Duck: See instructions for finishing chart for duck cardigan.

ELEPHANT:

For tail, with crochet hook and D, ch 1½"/4cm. Fasten off and

attach as indicated on chart.

For eye, use one strand of A and form french knot as

indicated on chart.

For ear, with crochet hook and E, ch 20. Spiral ch and tack

tog to form circle. Attach as indicated on chart.

counting sheep

❖ ❖ ❖

Materials

Tahki Yarns/Tahki • Stacy Charles, Inc., Cotton Classic II, 1¾oz/50g skeins, each approx 74yd/68m (cotton)

- *5 skeins in #2446 pink (A)*
- *1 skein each in #2712 green (B), #2001 white (C) and #2837 aqua (D)*
- *One pair each sizes 5 and 7 (3.75 and 4.5mm) needles OR SIZE TO OBTAIN GAUGE*
- *Stitch holder*

Sample is shown in size 18 months.

Skill level

Intermediate

BACK

Using basic pullover (page 12), cast on and work rib with B. Change to larger needles. With B, work in St st for 4 rows.

Beg grass chart

Row 1 (RS) Work 6 sts of grass chart 8 (9, 9) times, work first 4 (0, 2) sts once more. Cont as established until 2 rows of chart have been worked.

grass chart for pullover

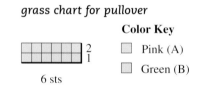

2
1

6 sts

Color Key

☐ Pink (A)

☐ Green (B)

Beg lamb chart

Row 1 (RS) Work 6 (7, 8) sts A, *work 11 sts of lamb chart, work 4 sts A; rep from *, ending last rep 5 (6, 7) sts A. Cont as established until 11 rows of chart have been worked. Cont in St st with A only and complete foll basic pullover.

lamb chart

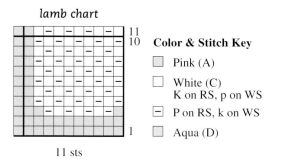

11 sts

Color & Stitch Key

☐   Pink (A)

☐   White (C)
     K on RS, p on WS

⊟   P on RS, k on WS

☐   Aqua (D)

FRONT

Work as for back until 11 rows of lamb chart have been worked. Cont in St st with A only and complete foll basic pullover.

SLEEVES

Cast on and work rib with B. Change to larger needles. With B, work in St st for 2 rows.

Beg grass chart

Row 1 (RS) Work 6 sts of grass chart 5 (5, 6) times, work first 4 (4, 0) sts once more. Cont as established until 2 rows of chart have been worked. Cont in St st with A only and complete foll basic pullover.

FINISHING

Complete foll basic pullover. Work neckband with A.

counting sheep

❖ ❖ ❖

Materials

Tahki Yarns/Tahki • Stacy Charles, Inc., Cotton Classic II,
1¾oz/50g skeins, each approx 74yd/68m (cotton)

- *1 skein each in #2446 pink (A) OR #2841 blue*
  (A), #2712 green (B) and #2001 white (C)
- *One pair each sizes 5 and 7 (3.75 and 4.5mm)*
  needles OR SIZE TO OBTAIN GAUGE
- *Tapestry needle*

Sample is shown in size 12 months.

Skill level

Intermediate

Note: Hat and mittens are worked in green with either pink or blue as A.

HAT

Cast on and work rib with B. Change to larger needles. With B, p 1 row.

Beg lamb chart for hat

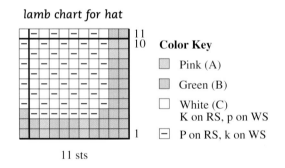

lamb chart for hat

Color Key

- ▨ Pink (A)
- ▨ Green (B)
- ☐ White (C)
  K on RS, p on WS
- ⊟ P on RS, k on WS

11 sts

Row 1 (RS) Work 6 (4) sts B, *work 11 sts of lamb chart, work 7(9) sts B; rep from *, ending last rep 6 (9) sts B. Cont as established until 11 rows of chart have been worked, With B, p 1 row.

Materials

Tahki Yarns/Tahki • Stacy Charles, Inc., Cotton Classic II, 1¾oz/50g skeins, each approx 74yd/68m (cotton)

- *Selected yarn #2446 pink or #2841 blue (A), #2712 green (B) and #2001 white (C)*
- *One pair each sizes 5 and 7 (3.75 and 4.5mm) needles OR SIZE TO OBTAIN GAUGE*
- *Tapestry needle*

Sample shown in size 12 months.

Skill level

Intermediate

Beg fence chart

Row 1 (RS) Work 3 sts of fence chart 25 (28) times, work first 2 (0) sts once more. Cont as established until 5 rows of chart have been worked. Cont in St st with A only and complete foll basic hat.

MITTENS

Cast on and work rib with B. Change to larger needles. Work 6 rows in st st with B. Work fence chart. With A, complete foll basic mittens.

fence chart

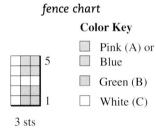

3 sts

Color Key
- ☐ Pink (A) or Blue
- ☐ Green (B)
- ☐ White (C)

big on brights

✦✦✦

Bold hues capture the vitality and spirit

found in children, and this energized

collection brims with color-charged knits

that will surely inspire.

red alert • feeling ducky • go fish! •
dairy land • all aboard • siren call

red alert

❖ ❖ ❖

Chase the chills away with these bear essentials.

A red-nosed polar bear motif and a

snowflake pattern decorate the hems;

plastic teddy bear buttons lend a dash of

whimsy to the cardigan.

Hats off to fashion! Jazz up an otherwise simple button-front cardigan and ribbed hat with some bright colors, bobble beaks and checkered border. The matching pillow features a knit-in duck motif against a rich purple backdrop.

feeling ducky

❖ ❖ ❖

go fish!

✦ ✦ ✦

He doesn't need to sail the Atlantic to know what lies on the floors of the deep blue sea. His pullover-and-hat set showcases a carefree school of fish with buttoned eyes swimming over bright white waves. Accent the ensemble with a snazzy hat and pair of mittens—you choose the design!

dairy land

✦ ✦ ✦

This is what I call grass roots! Featuring

chain-stitched ears and tails,

sprightly black-and-white cows graze

over a cheerful backdrop of blue and green.

Top the hat off with a bell and yarn

bows for a fanciful finish.

Your wee conductor is sure to impress the
fashion set at gymboree in a choo-choo-friendly
ensemble. Sew-on buttons make
terrific wheels—now let the good times roll!

all aboard

❖ ❖ ❖

siren call

❖ ❖ ❖

Your small tyke may not be extinguishing

any fires or rescuing cats out of trees just yet,

but he'll be the envy of all his playmates

in this winsome rough-and-tumble pullover.

The hat and mittens complete the look.

red alert

❖ ❖ ❖

Materials

Tahki Yarns/Tahki • Stacy Charles, Inc., Cotton Classic II,
1¾oz/50g skeins, each approx 74yd/68m (cotton)

- *6 skeins in #2997 red (A)*
- *1 skein in #2873 blue (C)*

Crystal Palace Chenille, 1¾oz/50g skeins, each
approx 98yd/88m (cotton)

- *1 skein in #2001 white (B)*
- *One pair each sizes 5 and 7 (3.75 and 4.5mm)*
  needles OR SIZE TO OBTAIN GAUGE
- *Crochet hook size G/6 (4mm)*
- *Tapestry needle*
- *Four ½"/13mm bear silhouette buttons*

Sample is shown in size 6 months.

Skill level

Intermediate

CARDIGAN BACK

Using basic cardigan (page 11), cast on and work rib with A. Change to larger needles. Work in St st for 2 rows.

Beg diamond chart

Row 1 (RS) Work 8 sts of diamond chart 6 (6, 7) times, work first 4 (6, 0) sts once more. Cont as established until 5 rows of chart have been worked. Cont in St st and A and complete foll basic cardigan.

diamond chart for cardigan

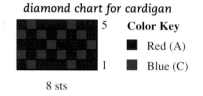

5

1

8 sts

Color Key
- ■ Red (A)
- ■ Blue (C)

RIGHT FRONT

Cast on and work rib with A. Change to larger needles. Work in St st for 2 rows.

Beg diamond chart

Row 1 (RS) Work 8 sts of diamond chart 3 times, work first 0 (1, 2) sts once more. Cont as established until 5 rows of chart have been worked. Work in St st for 4 rows with A.

Beg bear chart

Row 1 (WS) Work 6 (7, 8) sts A, work 13 sts of bear chart, work 5 sts A. Cont as established until 11 rows of chart have been worked. Cont in St st and A and complete foll basic cardigan.

bear chart for cardigan

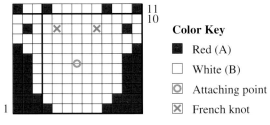

Color Key
- ■ Red (A)
- □ White (B)
- ◎ Attaching point
- ☒ French knot

13 sts

LEFT FRONT

Work as for right front, reversing placement of chart and all shaping.

RIGHT SLEEVE

Cast on and work rib with A. Change to larger needles. Work in St st for 2 rows.

Beg diamond chart

Row 1 (RS) Work 8 sts of diamond chart 4 times, work first 2 (2, 4) sts once more. Cont as established until 5 rows of chart have been worked. Work in St st for 2 rows with A.

Beg bear chart

Row 1 (WS) Work 18 (18, 20) sts A, work 12 sts of bear chart, work 4 sts A. Cont as established until 10 rows of chart have been worked, then work in St st and with A only, AT THE SAME TIME, complete foll basic cardigan.

LEFT SLEEVE

Work as for right sleeve, reversing placement of bear chart as foll: work 4 sts A, work 12 sts of bear chart, work 18 (18, 20) sts A.

FINISHING

Complete foll basic cardigan. Work bands with A. Sew buttons opposite buttonholes.

EMBELLISHMENTS

For eyes, use one strand of C and form French knots as indicated on chart.

For nose on fronts and sleeves, with crochet hook and A, ch 10 (8), fasten off. Spiral into circle and attach as indicated on chart.

HAT

Using basic hat (page 13), cast on and work rib with A. Change to larger needles.

Beg diamond chart

Row 1 (RS) Work 8 sts of diamond chart 9 (10) times, work first 5 (4) sts

diamond chart for hat

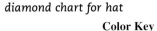

8 sts

Color Key
- ■ Red (A)
- ■ Blue (C)

once more. Cont as established until 3 rows of chart have been worked. Work in St st for 2 rows with A.

Beg bear chart

Row 1 (WS)

Work 33 (36) sts A, work 12 sts of bear chart, work 32 (36) sts A.

Cont as established until 10

bear chart for hat

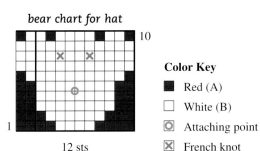

12 sts

Color Key
- ■ Red (A)
- □ White (B)
- ◎ Attaching point
- ☒ French knot

rows of chart have been worked, then work in St st and with A only, AT THE SAME TIME, complete foll basic hat.

FINISHING

Work embellishments as for bear cardigan.

For bow, with crochet hook and C, make a 13"/33cm chain. Tie in a bow and attach to center top with 2½"/6.5cm tails.

feeling ducky

❖ ❖ ❖

Materials

Tahki Yarns/Tahki • Stacy Charles, Inc., Cotton Classic II,
1¾oz/50g skeins, each approx 74yd/68m (cotton)

- *4 (5, 5) skeins in #2924 purple (A)*
- *3 skeins in #2764 green (B)*
- *1 skein each in #2871 blue (C), 2533 yellow (D)*
  and 2997 red (E)
- *One pair each sizes 5 and 7 (3.75 and 4.5mm)*
  needles OR SIZE TO OBTAIN GAUGE
- *Crochet hook size G/6 (4mm)*
- *Tapestry needle*
- *Four ½"/13mm buttons*

Sample is shown in size 12 months.

Skill level

Intermediate

STRIPE PATTERN

*4 rows A, 4 rows B; rep from * (8 rows) for stripe pat.

BACK

Using basic cardigan (page 11), cast on and work rib with B. Change to larger

needles.

Beg check chart

Row 1 (RS) Work 4 sts of check

chart 13 (13, 14) times, work 0 (2,

0) sts C. Cont as established until

4 rows of chart have been

check chart

Color Key
- Green (B)
- Blue (C)

4 sts

worked then work rows 1 and 2 once more. Cont in St st with A only and

complete foll basic cardigan.

RIGHT FRONT

Cast on and work rib with B. Change to larger needles.

Beg check chart

Row 1 (RS) Work 4 sts of check chart 6 times, work 0 (1, 2) sts C. Cont as established until 6 rows of chart have been worked.

Beg duck chart

Row 1 (RS) Work 7 sts A, work 10 sts of duck chart, work 7 (8, 9) sts A. Cont as established until 14 rows of chart have been worked. Cont in St st and A only and complete foll basic cardigan.

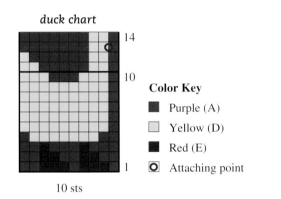

duck chart

Color Key
- ■ Purple (A)
- □ Yellow (D)
- ▨ Red (E)
- ◉ Attaching point

10 sts

LEFT FRONT

Work as for right front, reversing direction and placement of chart and all shaping.

SLEEVES

Cast on and work rib with B. Change to larger needles.

Beg check chart

Row 1 (RS) Work 4 sts of check chart 8 (8, 9) times, work 2 (2, 0) sts B. Cont as established until 4 rows of chart have been worked. Work in St st and stripe pat, complete foll basic

cardigan.

FINISHING

Complete foll basic cardigan. Work bands with B.

Sew 4 buttons to correspond to buttonholes.

EMBELLISHMENTS

For beak, with crochet hook and E, ch 7, fasten off. Spiral into circle and attach as indicated on chart.

HAT

Using basic hat (page 13), cast on and work rib with B. Change to larger needles.

Beg check chart

Row 1 (RS) Work 4 sts of check chart 19 (20) times, work 1 (4) sts B. Cont as established until 2 rows of chart have been worked.

Beg duck chart

Row 1 (RS) *Work 9 sts A, work 10 sts of duck chart; rep from *, end work 1 (8) sts A. Cont as established until 14 rows of chart have been worked. Cont in St st and complete foll basic hat as foll: 6 rows A, then work with E to end.

FINISHING

Work embellishment as for duck cardigan.

feeling ducky

❖ ❖ ❖

Materials

*Tahki Yarns/Tahki • Stacy Charles, Inc., Cotton Classic II,
1¾oz/50g skeins, each approx 74yd/68m (cotton)*

- 3 skeins in #2924 purple (A)
- 1 skein each in #2533 yellow (D) and #2997 red (E)
- 1 strand #2764 green (B)
- One pair size 7 (4.5mm) needles
  OR SIZE NEEDED TO OBTAIN GAUGE
- Three ½"/13mm red dome shank buttons
- Tapestry needle

Skill level

Intermediate

PILLOW

Cast on with A and work foll basic pillow through first turning ridge. Cont
with A and St st for 10 rows more.

Beg chart

Next row (RS) Work 10 sts A, work 27 sts of duck chart, work 9 sts A. Cont as
established until 40 rows of duck chart have been worked. Cont with A only
and work in St st for 9 rows more. Complete foll basic pillow.

FINISHING

Sew buttons opposite buttonholes.

For eye use one strand of B and form French knot as indicated on chart.

For wing, with D, cast on 13 sts. Work in St st for 4 rows, then dec 1 st each side every other row 5 times—3 sts. Cut yarn leaving a long

tail. Pull through rem sts and fasten off tightly. Attach as

indicated on chart.

duck chart for pillow

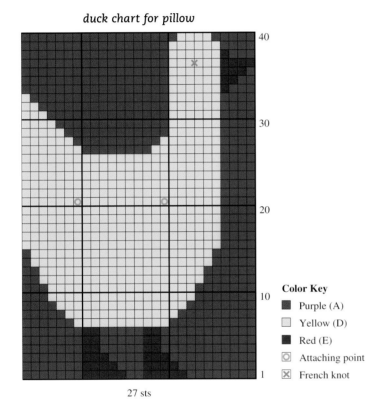

27 sts

Color Key

■ Purple (A)

□ Yellow (D)

■ Red (E)

◎ Attaching point

☒ French knot

go fish!

❖ ❖ ❖

Materials

Tahki Yarns/Tahki • Stacy Charles, Inc., Cotton Classic II,
1¾oz/50g skeins, each approx 74yd/68m (cotton)

- *6 skeins in #2871 blue (A)*
- *2 skeins in #2001 white (B)*
- *1 skein each in #2997 red (C), #2533 yellow (D),*
  #2764 green (E) and #2726 lime (F)
- *One pair each sizes 5 and 7 (3.75 and 4.5mm)*
  needles OR SIZE TO OBTAIN GAUGE
- *Tapestry needle*
- *Six ½"/13mm white buttons*

Sample is shown in size 18 months.

Skill level

Intermediate

STRIPE PATTERN

*4 rows B, 2 rows A; rep from * (6 rows) for stripe pat.

BACK

Using basic pullover (page 12), cast on and work rib with B. Change to larger needles. Work in St st for 4 rows.

Beg wave chart

Row 1 (RS) Work 6 sts wave chart 8 (9, 9) times, end work 4 (0, 2) sts A. Cont as established until 2 rows of chart have been worked. Work in St st for 4 rows with A.

Beg fish chart

Row 1 (RS) Work 2 (3, 4) sts A, *work 14 sts of fish chart, work 3 sts A; rep from *, end last rep 2 (3, 4) sts A, working fish as foll: F, C, D. Cont as established until 9 rows of chart have been worked. Work in St st and A only and complete foll basic pullover.

wave chart for pullover and hat

Color Key

■ Blue (A)
□ White (B)

6 sts

FRONT

Work as for back until wave chart is complete. Work in St st for 4 rows with A.

Beg fish chart

Row 1 (RS) Work 2 (3, 4) sts A, *work 14 sts of fish chart, work 3 sts A; rep from *, end last rep 2 (3, 4) sts A, working fish as foll: E, C, D. Cont as established until 9 rows of chart have been worked. Work in St st and A only and complete foll basic pullover.

SLEEVES

Cast on and work rib with B. Change to larger needles. Work in St st for 2 rows.

Beg wave chart

Row 1 (RS) Work 6 sts wave chart 5 (5, 6) times, end 4 (4, 0) sts A. Cont as established

fish charts for pullover

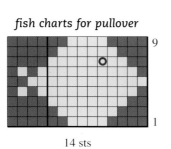

14 sts

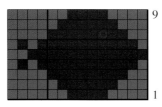

14 sts

fish chart for hat

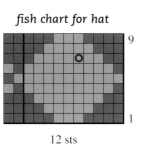

12 sts

Color Key

■ Blue (A)
■ Red (C)
□ Yellow (D)
▨ Green (E)
□ Lime (F)
 Attaching point

until 2 rows of chart have been worked. Work in St st and complete foll basic pullover.

FINISHING

Complete foll basic pullover. Work neckband with A. Attach buttons as indicated on chart.

HAT

Cast on and work rib with A. Change to larger needles. Work in St st for 2 rows.

Beg fish chart

Row 1 (RS) Work 5 (9) sts A, *work 12 sts of fish chart, work 6 sts A; rep from *, end last rep 6 (9) sts A, working fish as foll: F, C, E, D. Cont as established until 9 rows of chart have been worked. Work in St st for 2 rows with A. Cont in St st and stripe pat and complete foll basic hat.

FINISHING

Attach buttons as indicated on chart.

go fish!

❖ ❖ ❖

Materials

Tahki Yarns/Tahki • Stacy Charles, Inc., Cotton Classic II, 1¾oz/50g skeins, each approx 74yd/68m (cotton)

- *1 skein each in #2882 periwinkle (A), #2002 black (H) and #2001 white (I)*
- *Small amounts in #2459 fuchsia (B), #2815 blue (C), #2726 green (D), #2401 orange (E), #2533 yellow (F) and #2997 red (G)*
- *One pair each sizes 5 and 7 (3.75 and 4.5mm) needles OR SIZE TO OBTAIN GAUGE*
- *Crochet hook size G/6 (4mm)*
- *Tapestry needle*

Skill level

Intermediate

STRIPE PATTERN FOR DOT HAT

*2 rows H, 2 rows I; rep from * (4 rows) for stripe pat.

STRIPE PATTERN FOR SQUIGGLE HAT AND MITTENS

*2 rows I, 2 rows H; rep from * (4 rows) for stripe pat.

DOT HAT

Using basic hat (page 13) cast on and work rib with A. Change to larger needles. Work in St st for 4 rows with A.

Beg dot chart for hat

dot charts for hat

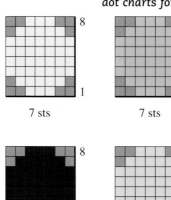

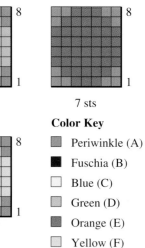

7 sts   7 sts   7 sts

7 sts   7 sts

Color Key

- ▦ Periwinkle (A)
- ■ Fuschia (B)
- ☐ Blue (C)
- ▨ Green (D)
- ▤ Orange (E)
- ☐ Yellow (F)

Row 1 (RS) Work 7 sts A, *work 7 sts of dot chart, work 7 sts A; rep from *, end 0 (7) sts A, working dots as foll: C, D, E, B, F. Cont as established until 8 rows of chart have been worked. Cont in St st and complete foll basic hat as foll: with A, work in St st for 7 rows, then work in stripe pat to the end.

FINISHING

With crochet hook and A, make a 13"/33cm chain. Tie in a bow and attach to center top with 2½"/6.5cm tails.

SQUIGGLE HAT

Cast on and work rib with H. Change to larger needles. Work in St st and stripe pat and complete foll basic hat.

FINISHING

With crochet hook, work chain-stitch in varied colors, foll photo and diagram for placement and shape.

MITTENS (THUMBLESS)

Using basic mitten (page 14), cast on and work rib with H. Change to larger needles. Cont in St st and stripe pat and complete foll basic thumbless mittens.

squiggle chart for hat and mittens

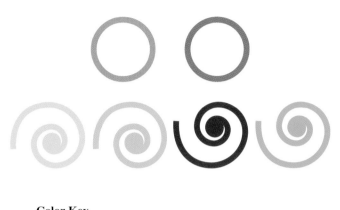

Color Key

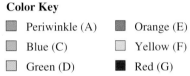

▦ Periwinkle (A)	▦ Orange (E)
▦ Blue (C)	▦ Yellow (F)
▦ Green (D)	■ Red (G)

FINISHING

With crochet hook, work chain-stitch in A and D, foll photo and diagram for placement and shape.

dairy land

❖ ❖ ❖

Materials

Tahki Yarns/Tahki • Stacy Charles, Inc., Cotton Classic II,
1¾oz/50g skeins, each approx 74yd/68m (cotton)

- 5 skeins in #2815 blue (A)
- 2 skeins in #2726 green (B)
- 1 skein each in #2001 white (C), #2002 black (D)
  and #2533 yellow (F)
- Small amount in #2459 pink (E)
- One pair each sizes 5 and 7 (3.75 and 4.5mm)
  needles OR SIZE TO OBTAIN GAUGE
- Crochet hook size G/6 (4mm)
- Tapestry needle
- Four ⅝"/15mm daisy buttons
- Silver bell on shank ½"/13mm (may also be
  embroidered using silver embroidery thread)

Sample is shown in size 12 months.

Skill level

Intermediate

BACK

Using basic cardigan (page 11), cast on and work rib with B. Change to larger needles. Work in St st for 4 rows.

Beg grass border

Row 1 (RS) *Work 1 st A, work 1 st B; rep from *, end work 2 sts A. Cont as established for 1 row more. Cont in St st and A and complete foll basic cardigan.

RIGHT FRONT

Using basic cardigan (page 11), cast on and work rib with B. Change to larger needles. Work in St st for 4 rows.

Beg grass border

Row 1 (RS) *Work 1 st A, work 1 st B; rep from *, end work 2 sts A. Cont as established for 1 row more.

Beg cow chart

Row 1 (RS) Work 5 sts A, work 15 sts of cow chart, work 4 (5, 6) sts A. Cont

cow chart for cardigan and afghan

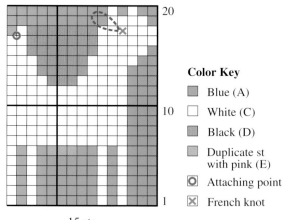

15 sts

Color Key

- ⬛ Blue (A)
- ⬜ White (C)
- ⬛ Black (D)
- ⬛ Duplicate st with pink (E)
- ⊙ Attaching point
- ⊠ French knot

as established until 20 rows of chart have been worked. Cont in St st and A and complete foll basic cardigan.

LEFT FRONT

Work as for right front, reversing direction and placement of chart and all shaping.

SLEEVES

Cast on and work rib with B. Change to larger needles. Work in St st for 2 rows.

Beg grass border

Row 1 (RS) *Work 1 st A, work 1 st B; rep from * to end. Cont as established for 1 row more. Cont in St st and A and complete foll basic cardigan.

FINISHING

Complete foll basic cardigan. Work bands with A, working buttonhole band on left front and button band on right front. Sew buttons opposite buttonholes.

EMBELLISHMENTS

For eyes, use one strand of D and form French knots as indicated on chart

For tail, with crochet hook and C, make a 1"/2.5cm chain. Fasten off and attach as indicated on chart.

For ear, with crochet hook and C, ch 8, fasten off. Sew center tog and attach as indicated on chart.

For utters, duplicate stitch with E as indicated on chart.

GRASS

For fronts and back, with B, cut 3½"/9cm long strands for fringe. Pull through and knot. Trim grass to 1¼"/3cm.

For sleeves, with B, cut 3"/7.5cm long strands for fringe. Attach and trim grass to 1"/2.5cm.

HAT

Using basic hat (page 13), cast on and work rib with B. Change to larger needles. Work in St st for 2 rows.

Beg grass border

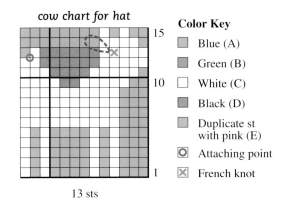

cow chart for hat

Color Key
- Blue (A)
- Green (B)
- □ White (C)
- Black (D)
- Duplicate st with pink (E)
- ⊙ Attaching point
- ☒ French knot

13 sts

Row 1 (RS) *Work 1 st A, work 1 st B; rep from *, end work 1 st A. Cont as established for 1 row more.

Beg cow chart

Row 1 (RS) Work 32 (35) sts A, work 13 sts of cow chart, work 32 (36) sts A. Cont as established until 15 rows of chart have been worked, At the same time, complete foll basic hat. When chart is complete, work 6 rows A, work in F to end.

FINISHING

Work embellishments as for cow cardigan.

For grass, work as for sleeves on cardigan.

For bow, with crochet hook and F, make a 13"/33cm chain. Tie in a bow and attach to center top with 2½"/6.5cm tails.

For bell, attach at top of hat (optional: embroider bell using silver thread).

dairy land

❖ ❖ ❖

Materials

Tahki Yarns/Tahki • Stacy Charles, Inc., Cotton Classic II, 1¾oz/50g skeins, each approx 74yd/68m (cotton)

- *8 skeins in #2815 blue (A)*
- *7 skeins in #2726 green (B)*
- *1 skein each in #2001 white (C) and #2002 black (D)*
- *Small amount in #2459 pink (E)*
- *Size 7 (4.5mm) circular needle, 32"/80cm long OR SIZE TO OBTAIN GAUGE*
- *Crochet hook size G/6 (4mm)*
- *Silver bell on shank ½"/13mm (may also be embroidered using silver embroidery thread)*

Afghan measures approx 28" x 38"/71cm x 96.5cm.

Skill level

Intermediate

Notes

1 Work blocks in St st with separate balls of yarn for each block. Twist yarns on WS to prevent holes.

2 4-st garter borders extend lengthwise on each side.

3 Each block is 29 sts x 36 rows

AFGHAN

With A, cast on 124 sts. Work in garter st for 1"/2.5cm.

Row 1 (RS) Work 4 sts in garter st with A, work blocks in St st, foll diagram for placement, work last 4 sts in garter st with A. Cont as established until all blocks have been worked. With A, work in garter st for 1"/2.5cm. Bind off.

SOLID BLOCK

Work 29 sts and 36 rows using A or B.

STRIPE BLOCK 1

Work on 29 sts as foll 36 rows: [4 rows A, 4 rows B] 4 times, 4 rows A.

STRIPE BLOCK 2

Work on 29 sts as foll 36 rows: [4 rows B, 4 rows A] 4 times, 4 rows B.

COW BLOCK

Work 29 sts and 36 rows as foll:

Rows 1 to 8 St st with A.

Rows 9 to 28 Work 20 rows of cow chart as foll: 7 sts A, 15 sts cow chart, 7 sts A.

Rows 29 to 36 St st with A.

cow chart for afghan

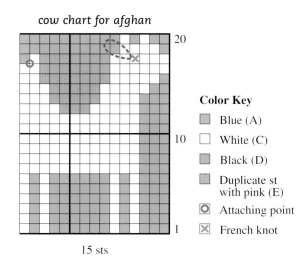

Color Key

- ▨ Blue (A)
- ☐ White (C)
- ▨ Black (D)
- ▨ Duplicate st with pink (E)
- ◉ Attaching point
- ☒ French knot

15 sts

FINISHING

For eyes, use one strand of D and form French knots as indicated on chart.

For tail, with crochet hook and C, make a 1"/2.5cm chain. Fasten off and attach as indicated on chart.

For ear, with crochet hook and C, ch 8, fasten off. Sew cen-ter tog and attach as indicated on chart.

For utters, duplicate stitch with E as indicated on chart.

For grass, with B, cut 3½"/9cm long strands for fringe. Pull through and knot fringe. Trim grass to 1¼"/3cm.

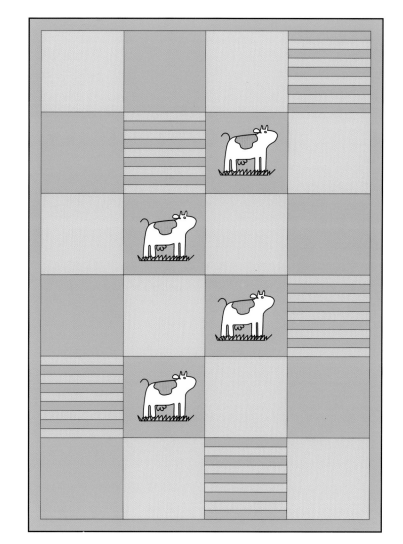

all aboard

❖ ❖ ❖

Materials

Tahki Yarns/Tahki • Stacy Charles, Inc., Cotton Classic II, 1¾oz/50g skeins, each approx 74yd/68m (cotton)

- *6 skeins in #2871 blue (A)*
- *1 skein each in #2997 red (B), #2533 yellow (C) and #2764 green (D)*
- *One pair each sizes 5 and 7 (3.75 and 4.5mm) needles OR SIZE TO OBTAIN GAUGE*
- *Tapestry needle*
- *Four ½"/13mm shank buttons (2 red and 2 yellow)*
- *Eight ½"/13mm wheel buttons for cardigan*
- *Eight ½"/13mm wheel buttons for hat*

Sample is shown in size 12 months.

Skill level

Intermediate

BACK

Using basic cardigan (page 11), cast on and work rib with A. Change to larger needles. Work in St st for 4 rows.

Beg track chart

Row 1 (RS) Work 6 sts of track chart 8 (9, 9) times, work first 4 (0, 2) sts once more. Cont as established until 4 rows of chart have been worked. Cont in St st with A and complete foll basic cardigan.

track chart for cardigan and hat

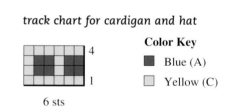

4

1

6 sts

Color Key

■ Blue (A)

□ Yellow (C)

RIGHT FRONT

Cast on and work rib with A. Change to larger needles. Work in St st for 4 rows.

Beg track chart

Row 1 (RS) Work 6 sts of track chart 4 times, work first 0 (1, 2) sts once more. Cont as established until 4 rows of chart have been worked. K 1 row A.

Beg train chart

Row 1 (WS) Work 7 sts A, work 11 sts of train chart, work 6 (7, 8) sts A. Cont as established until 8 rows of chart have been worked. Cont in St st and A only and complete foll basic cardigan.

train charts for cardigan

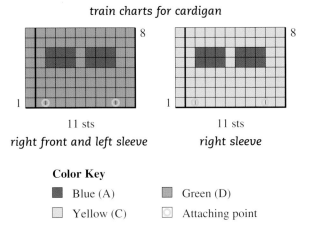

11 sts
right front and left sleeve

11 sts
right sleeve

Color Key
■ Blue (A) ■ Green (D)
□ Yellow (C) ▣ Attaching point

engine chart left front

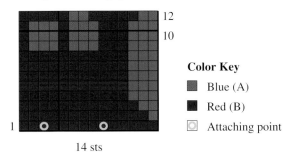

12
10

1

14 sts

Color Key
■ Blue (A)
■ Red (B)
▣ Attaching point

LEFT FRONT

Cast on and work rib with A. Change to larger needles. Work in St st for 4 rows.

Beg track chart

Row 1 (RS) Work 6 sts of track chart 4 times, work first 0 (1, 2) sts once more. Cont as established until 4 rows of chart have been worked. K 1 row A.

Beg engine chart

Row 1 (WS) Work 4 (5, 6) sts A, work 14 sts of engine chart, work 6 sts A. Cont as established until 12 rows of chart have been worked. Cont in St st and A only and complete foll basic cardigan.

RIGHT SLEEVE

Cast on and work rib with A. Change to larger needles. Work in St st for 2 rows.

Beg track chart

Row 1 (RS) Work 6 sts of track chart 5 (5, 6) times, work first 4 (4, 0) sts once more. Cont as established until 4 rows of chart have been worked. K 1 row A.

Beg train chart

Row 1 (WS) Work 18 (18, 20) sts A, work 11 sts of train chart, work 5 sts A. Cont as established until 6 rows of chart have been worked, then work in St st and with A only, AT THE SAME TIME, complete foll basic cardigan.

LEFT SLEEVE

Work as for right sleeve, reversing placement of train chart as foll: Work 5 sts A, work 11 sts of train chart, work 18 (18, 20) sts A.

all aboard

❖ ❖ ❖

FINISHING

Complete foll basic cardigan. Work bands with A, working buttonhole band on left front and button band on right front.

Sew buttons opposite buttonholes.

EMBELLISHMENTS

Attach wheel buttons as indicated on chart.

HAT

Using basic hat (page 13), cast on and work rib with A.

Change to larger needles.

Beg track chart

Row 1 (RS) Work 6 sts of track chart 12 (14) times, work first 5 (0) sts once more. Cont as established until 4 rows of chart have been worked. K 1 row A.

Beg engine and train charts

Row 1 (WS) Work 6 (9) sts A, work 11 sts of engine chart, *work 7 (9) sts A, work 11 sts of train chart (working trains in D, B and C); rep from *, end last rep work 6 (4) sts A. Work as

established until all 9 rows of engine chart and 6 rows of train chart (working 3 more rows with A) have been worked, AT THE SAME TIME, complete foll basic hat as foll: 8 rows A, then work in B to the end.

FINISHING

Attach wheel buttons as indicated on chart.

engine chart for hat

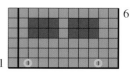

Color Key
■ Blue (A)
■ Red (B)
◎ Attaching point

11 sts

train charts for hat

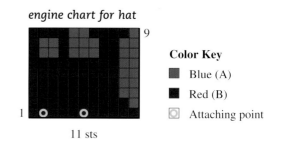

11 sts   11 sts

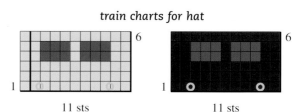

11 sts

siren call

Materials

Tahki Yarns/Tahki • Stacy Charles, Inc., Cotton Classic II,
1¾oz/50g skeins, each approx 74yd/68m (cotton)

- *4 skeins each in #2997 red (A) and #2002*
  black (B)
- *1 skein in #2001 white (C)*
- *One pair each sizes 5 and 7 (3.75 and 4.5mm)*
  needles OR SIZE TO OBTAIN GAUGE
- *Tapestry needle*
- *Four ½"/13mm wheel buttons for pullover*
- *Six ½"/13mm wheel buttons for hat*

Sample is shown in size 18 months.

Skill level

Intermediate

STRIPE PATTERN FOR FRONT AND BACK

*4 rows A, 4 rows B; rep from * (8 rows) for stripe pat.

STRIPE PATTERN FOR SLEEVES AND MITTENS

*4 rows B, 4 rows A; rep from * (8 rows) for stripe pat.

BACK

Using basic pullover (page 12), cast on and work rib with A. Change to larger

needles. Work in St st for 4 rows.

Beg check chart

Row 1 (RS) Work 4 sts of

check chart 13 (13, 14) times,

work 0 (2, 0) sts A. Cont as

established until 4 rows of

chart have been worked. Work in St st with B for 12 rows.

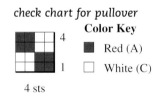

check chart for pullover

Color Key
- ■ Red (A)
- □ White (C)

4 sts

siren call

❖ ❖ ❖

Next row (RS) Work 5 (6, 7) sts B, *work 2 sts C, work 6 sts B; rep from *, end last rep 5 (6, 7) sts B. Work as established for 1 row more, then work 2 rows C. Cont in St st and stripe pat for back and complete foll basic pullover.

FRONT

Work as back until 1 row of B above check chart.

Beg fire truck chart

Row 1 (WS) Work 8 (9, 10) sts B, *work 14 sts of fire truck chart, work 8 sts B; rep from *, end last rep 8 (9, 10) sts B. Cont as established until 8 rows of chart have been worked. Work in St st for 3 rows with B.

Next row (WS) Work 5 (6, 7) sts B, *work 2 sts C, work 6 sts B; rep from *, end last rep 5 (6, 7) sts B. Work as established for 1 row more, then work 2 rows C. Cont in St st and stripe pat for front and complete foll basic pullover.

SLEEVES

Cast on and work rib with A. Change to larger needles. Work in St st and stripe pat for sleeves and complete foll basic pullover.

FINISHING

Complete foll basic pullover. Work neckband with A. Attach buttons as indicated on chart.

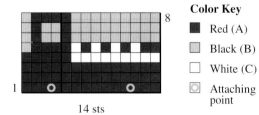

fire truck chart for pullover

1 — 8

14 sts

Color Key

■ Red (A)

▨ Black (B)

□ White (C)

◉ Attaching point

HAT

Using basic hat (page 13), cast on and work rib with A. Change to larger needles.

Beg check chart

Row 1 (RS) Work 4 sts of check chart 19 (21) times, work 1 (0) sts A. Cont as established until 4 rows of chart have been worked. K 1 row B.

check chart for hat

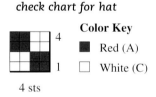

4 sts

Beg fire truck chart

Row 1 (WS) *Work 9 (11) sts B, work 14 sts of fire truck chart; rep from *, end work 8 (9) sts B. Cont as established until 8 rows of chart have been worked. Work in St st for 3 rows with B. Cont in St st and complete foll basic hat as foll:

*Work 6 sts B, work 2 sts C; rep from *, end 5 (4) sts B. Work as established for 1 row more, then work 6 rows C, then A until end of piece.

fire truck chart for hat

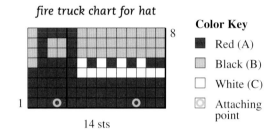

14 sts

FINISHING

Attach buttons as indicated on chart.

MITTENS

Using basic mitten (page 14) loosely cast on and work rib with A. Change to larger needles. Work in St st and stripe pat for mittens and complete foll basic mittens.

neutral zone

❖ ❖ ❖

A muted palette of neutral colors makes
for fuss-free coordination. These
creations are designed with your child in
mind; your biggest dilemma is to decide
which to knit first.

*farm fresh • bunny hop •
winter wonderland • feeling sheepish*

At the first sign of winter, these styles

will keep your loved one toasty all season long.

A red decorative fence adds a punch to a muted

two-toned sheep pullover-and-cap set; while a

chain stitch wing, loose waddle and a button

eye lend verve to the rooster sweater.

farm fresh

❖ ❖ ❖

bunny hop

What's up, Doc? Sprucing up a basic silhouette

is as easy as 1-2-3: just knit a fuzzy bunny

motif on a soft tweedy blue cardigan.

Rabbit ears are stitched separately,

then sewn on.

Northern exposure—Use the same basic pattern to create a bear or reindeer sweater. The knit-in animal motifs are embellished with embroidered and sewn-on accents.

winter wonderland

❖ ❖ ❖

feeling sheepish

❖ ❖ ❖

Dress your tyke and outfit your home at the same time with this coordinating set. It includes a button-front cardigan, easy-fit hat and mittens, striped afghan and sheep pillow— all in matching colors.

farm fresh

❖ ❖ ❖

Materials

Brown Sheep NatureSpun Worsted,

3½oz/100g each approx 245yd/224m (wool)

- *2 skeins in #N91 beige (A)*
- *1 skein each in #N46 red (B) and #601 black (C)*
- *One pair each sizes 5 and 7 (3.75 and 4.5mm) needles OR SIZE TO OBTAIN GAUGE*
- *Crochet hook size G/6 (4mm)*
- *Tapestry needle*
- *One ½"/13mm ecru 4-hole flat button*

Sample is shown in size 12 months.

Skill level

Intermediate

BACK

Using basic pullover (page 12), cast on with B and work 1 row in rib. Cont rib with A. Change to larger needles. Work in St st and A only and complete foll basic pullover.

FRONT

Cast on and work rib as for back. Change to larger needles. Work in St st for 4 rows.

Beg hen chart

Row 1 (RS) Work 12 (13, 14) sts A, work 28 sts of hen chart, work 12 (13, 14) sts A. Cont as established until 37 rows of chart have been worked. Cont in St st

hen chart

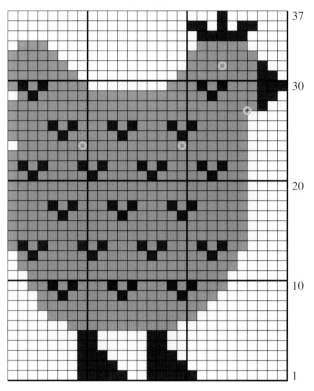

37
30
20
10
1

28 sts

Color Key

☐ Beige (A)

■ Red (B)

▨ Black (C)

◉ Attaching point

with A only and complete foll basic pullover.

SLEEVES

Cast on and work rib as for back. Change to larger needles.

Work in St st and A, complete foll basic pullover.

FINISHING

Complete foll basic pullover. Work neckband with A,

working last rib row in B. Bind off in B.

EMBELLISHMENTS

For eye, use C and sew on button as indicated on

chart, foll photo.

For wattle, with crochet hook and B, chain 10, fasten off.

Fold in half and sew tog, attach as indicated on chart.

For wing, with larger needles and C, cast on 12 sts. Work in

St st for 4 rows. Dec 1 st each side on next row, then every

other row 3 times—4 sts. Cut yarn, leaving a long tail. Pull

through rem sts and fasten off tightly. Attach as indicated

on chart, leaving lower edge loose. With B, chain-st around

lower edge of wing.

farm fresh

❖ ❖ ❖

Materials

Brown Sheep Lambs Pride Worsted

4oz/113g each approx 190y/173m (wool/mohair)

- *2 skeins in #M03 lt grey (B)*
- *1 skein each in #M04 charcoal (A), #M10 ecru (C) and #M181 brick red (D)*
- *One pair each sizes 5 and 7 (3.75 and 4.5mm) needles OR SIZE TO OBTAIN GAUGE*
- *Tapestry needle*

Sample is shown in size 12 months.

Skill level

Intermediate

PULLOVER

BACK

Using basic pullover (page 12), cast on and work rib with A. Change to larger
needles. Work in St st for 18 rows.

Beg fence chart

Row 1 (RS) Work 6 sts of fence chart 8 (9, 9) times, work first 4 (0, 2) sts
once more.

Cont as established until 5 rows of chart have been worked. Work in St st and
B only and complete foll basic pullover.

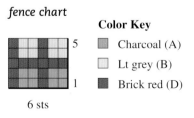

fence chart

5

1

6 sts

Color Key

▨ Charcoal (A)

☐ Lt grey (B)

▨ Brick red (D)

FRONT

Cast on and work rib with A. Change to larger needles. Work in St st for 4 rows.

Beg sheep chart

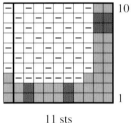

sheep chart

10

1

11 sts

Color Key

- ▢ Charcoal (A)
- ▢ Off-white (C)
  K on RS, p on WS
- ⊟ P on RS, k on WS
- ▢ Brick red (D)

Row 1 (RS) Work 4 (5, 6) sts A, *work 11 sts of sheep chart, work 5 sts A; rep from *, end last rep sts 5 (6, 7) sts A. Cont as established until 10 rows of chart have been worked. Work in St st with A for 4 rows.

Beg fence chart

Row 1 (RS) Work 6 sts of fence chart 8 (9, 9) times, work first 4 (0, 2) sts once more.

Cont as established until 5 rows of chart have been worked. Work in St st with B only and complete foll basic pullover.

SLEEVES

Cast on and work rib with B. Change to larger needles. Work in St st and B, complete foll basic pullover.

FINISHING

Complete foll basic pullover. Work neckband with B.

HAT

Using basic hat (page 13), cast on and work rib with A. Change to larger needles. Work in St st for 1 row.

Beg lamb chart

Row 1 (RS) Work 6 (4) sts A, *work 11 sts of lamb chart, work 7 (9) sts A; rep from *, end last rep 6 (9) sts A. Cont as established until 10 rows of chart have been worked. Work in St st with A for 1 row.

Beg fence chart

Row 1 (WS) Work 6 sts of fence chart 12 (14) times, work first 5 (0) sts once more.

Cont as established until 5 rows of chart have been worked. Cont in St st and B only and complete foll basic hat.

bunny hop

❖ ❖ ❖

Materials

Tahki Yarns/Tahki • Stacy Charles, Inc., New Tweed
1¾oz/50g each approx 103yd/92m
(wool/silk/cotton/viscose)

• *4 skeins in #018 purple (A)*

Tahki Yarns/Tahki • Stacy Charles, Inc., Jolie
.88oz/25g each approx 108yd/97m (angora/wool)

• *1 skein in #5001 white (B)*

• *Size 5 and 7 (3.75 and 4.5mm) needles OR SIZE*
  TO OBTAIN GAUGE

• *Tapestry needle*

• *Crochet hook size G/6 (4mm)*

• *Four ½"/13mm white pearl-cluster shank*
  buttons

Sample is shown in size 6 months.

Skill level

Intermediate

CARDIGAN

BACK

Using basic cardigan (page 11), cast on and work rib with A. Change to larger

needles. Cont in St st with A only and complete foll basic cardigan.

RIGHT FRONT

Cast on and work rib with A. Change to larger needles. Work in St st

for 4 rows.

Beg bunny chart

Row 1 (RS) Work 4 sts A, work 15 sts of bunny chart, work 5 (6, 7) sts A. Cont

as established until 16 rows of chart have been worked. Cont with A only and

complete foll basic cardigan.

bunny chart for pullover

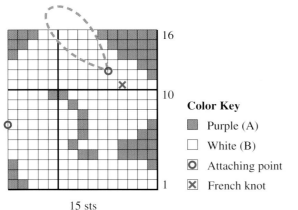

16

10

Color Key
- ■ Purple (A)
- □ White (B)
- ◉ Attaching point
- ✖ French knot

1

15 sts

LEFT FRONT

Work as for right front, reversing direction and placement of chart and all shaping.

SLEEVES

Cast on and work rib with A. Change to larger needles.

Working in St st with A only, complete foll basic cardigan.

FINISHING

Complete foll basic cardigan. Work neckband and front bands with A.

Sew buttons opposite buttonholes.

EMBELLISHMENTS

For eyes use one strand of A and form French knot as indicated on chart.

For ears, with crochet hook and B, ch 16, fasten off. Fold in half and sew center. Attach one side as indicated on chart.

For tail, with crochet hook and B, ch 16, fasten off. Spiral into circle and attach as indicated on chart.

HAT

Using basic hat (page 13), cast on and work rib with A. Change to larger needles. Work in St st with A for 2 rows.

Beg bunny chart for hat

bunny chart for hat

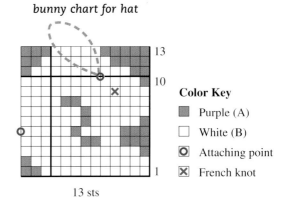

13

10

Color Key
- ■ Purple (A)
- □ White (B)
- ◉ Attaching point
- ✖ French knot

1

13 sts

Row 1 (RS) Work 32 (36) sts A, work 13 sts of bunny chart, work 32 (35) sts A. Cont as established until 13 rows of chart have been worked Cont in St st with A only and complete foll basic hat.

EMBELLISHMENTS

Work as for bunny cardigan.

bunny hop

❖ ❖ ❖

Materials

Tahki Yarns/Tahki • Stacy Charles, Inc., New Tweed 1¾oz/50g each approx 103yd/92m (wool/silk/cotton/viscose)

- *2 skeins in #018 purple (A)*

Tahki Yarns/Tahki • Stacy Charles, Inc., Jolie .88oz/25g each approx 108 yd/97m (angora/wool)

- *1 skein in #5001 white (B)*
- *One pair each sizes 5 and 7 (3.75 and 4.5mm) needles OR SIZE TO OBTAIN GAUGE*
- *Crochet hook size G/6 (4mm)*
- *Tapestry needle*
- *Three ½"/13mm white pearl-cluster shank buttons*
- *10"/25.5cm square pillow form by Airtex*

Sample is shown in size 12 months.

Skill level

Intermediate

PILLOW

Using basic pillow (page 14), cast on with A. Foll basic pillow through first turning ridge. Cont with A and St st for 11 rows more.

Beg bunny pillow chart

Row 1 (RS) Work 9 sts A, work 28 sts of bunny pillow chart, work 9 sts A. Cont as established until 33 rows of chart have been worked. Cont in St st with A only and work 14 rows more. Complete foll basic pillow.

FINISHING

Sew buttons opposite buttonholes.

bunny chart for pillow

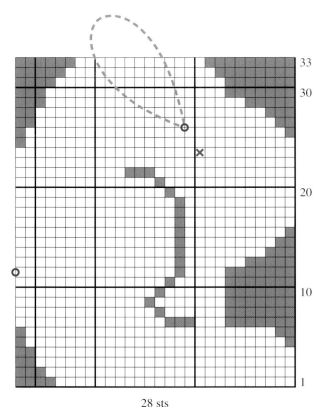

28 sts

Color Key

- ▦ Purple (A)
- ☐ White (B)
- ◎ Attaching point
- ☒ French knot

EMBELLISHMENTS

For eyes, use A and form French knots as indicated on chart.

For ear, with B, cast on 3 sts. Work in St st, inc 1 st each side every other row twice—7 sts. Work even until piece measures 2½"/6.5cm, then dec 1 st each side every other row twice—3 sts. Cut yarn and pull through rem sts, fasten off. With B, embroider chain st around ear and attach as indicated on chart, leaving side and top open.

For tail, with B, ch 12, fasten off. Spiral into circle and attach as indicated on chart.

winter wonderland

❖ ❖ ❖

Materials

Tahki Yarns/Tahki • Stacy Charles, Inc., Cotton Classic II,
1¾oz/50g skeins, each approx 74yd/68m (cotton)

- *5 skeins in #2001 tan (A)*
- *2 skeins in #2203 brown (B)*
- *1 skein each in #2317 dk brown (C) and #2003 ecru (D)*
- *One pair each sizes 5 and 7 (3.75 and 4.5mm) needles OR SIZE TO OBTAIN GAUGE*
- *Crochet hook size G/6 (4mm)*
- *Tapestry needle*
- *Small amount fiberfill*

Sample is shown in size 12 months.

Skill level

Intermediate

PULLOVER

STRIPE PATTERN

*2 rows B, 4 rows A; rep from * (6 rows) for stripe pat.

BACK

Using basic pullover (page 12), cast on and work rib with A. Change to larger needles. Work in St st and A only and complete foll basic pullover.

FRONT

Cast on and work rib with A. Change to larger needles. Work in St st with A for 4 rows.

Beg bear chart

Row 1 (RS) Work 12 (13, 14) sts A, work 28 sts of bear chart, work 12 (13, 14) sts A. Cont as established until 36 rows of chart have been worked. Work in St st and A only and complete foll basic pullover.

bear chart for pullover

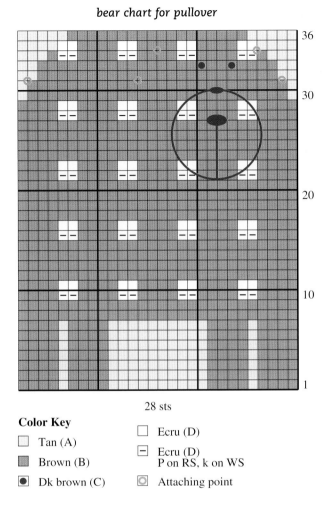

28 sts

Color Key

☐ Tan (A)

▨ Brown (B)

◉ Dk brown (C)

☐ Ecru (D)

⊟ Ecru (D)
   P on RS, k on WS

◎ Attaching point

SLEEVES

Cast on and work rib with A. Change to larger needles.

Working in St st and stripe pat, complete foll basic pullover.

FINISHING

Complete foll basic pullover. Work neckband with A.

EMBELLISHMENTS

For eyes, use one strand of C and form French knots as indicated on chart.

For ears, (make 2) with B, cast on 4 sts. Work in St st for 4 rows. Cut yarn, leaving a long tail and thread through rem sts. Pull tight to gather and fasten off. Attach as indicated on chart, leave top loose.

For tail, with crochet hook and B, chain 1"/2.5cm, fasten off. Sew center tog and attach as indicated on chart.

For muzzle, with B, cast on 4 sts. Work in St st, inc 1 st each side every other row 3 times—10 sts. Work even for 4 rows. Dec 1 st each side on next row, then every other row twice more—4 sts. Bind off.

For nose, with C, work French knot for nose on muzzle and chain st nose outline as indicated on chart. Attach muzzle as indicated on chart, leaving small opening for fiberfill. Stuff and sew closed. Chain stitch around in B.

HAT

Using basic hat (page 13), cast on and work rib with A. Change to larger needles. Work in St st and stripe pat, and complete foll basic hat.

winter wonderland

❖ ❖ ❖

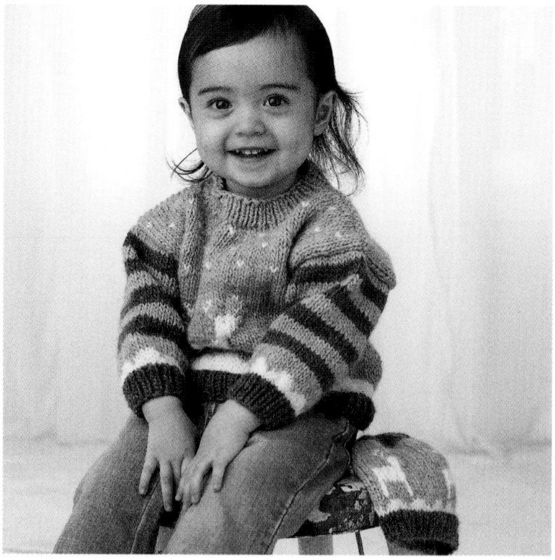

Materials

Brown Sheep Lambs Pride Worsted

4oz/113g each approx 190yd/173m (wool/mohair)

- *2 skeins in #M01 beige (A)*
- *1 skein each in #M02 brown (B) and #M10 ecru (C)*
- *One pair each sizes 5 and 7 (3.75 and 4.5mm) needles OR SIZE TO OBTAIN GAUGE*
- *Tapestry needle*
- *Three 3/8"/10mm 2-holed wooden buttons for pullover*
- *Four 3/8"/10mm 2-holed wooden buttons for hat*

Sample is shown in size 18 months.

Skill level

Intermediate

PULLOVER

STRIPE PATTERN

*4 rows A, 4 rows B; rep from * (8 rows) for stripe pat.

BACK

Using basic pullover (page 12), cast on and work rib with B. Change to larger needles.

Beg snow chart

Row 1 (RS) Work 6 sts of snow chart 8 (9, 9) times, work first 4 (0, 2) sts once more. Cont as established until 6 rows of chart have been worked. Work in St st and A only and complete foll basic pullover.

snow chart for pullover

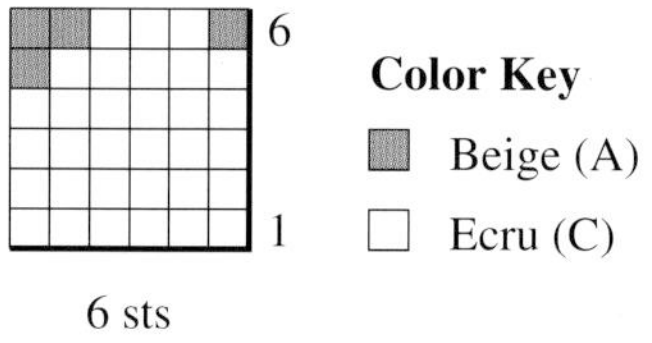

FRONT

Work as for back through snow chart.

Beg reindeer chart

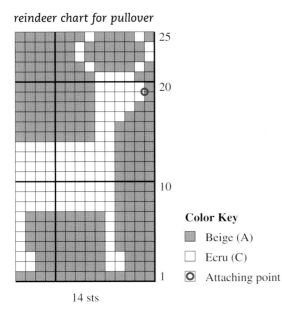

reindeer chart for pullover

14 sts

Color Key

- ▨ Beige (A)
- ☐ Ecru (C)
- ⊙ Attaching point

Row 1 (RS) Work 1 (2, 3) sts A, work *14 sts of reindeer chart, work 4 sts A; rep from *, end last rep 1 (2, 3) sts A. Cont as established until 25 rows of chart have been worked. Work in St st and A for 8 rows.

Beg falling snow chart

Row 1 (RS) Work 8 (9, 10) sts A, work 37 sts of falling snow chart, work 7 (8, 9) sts A. Cont as established until 21 rows of chart have been worked. Work in St st with A only and complete foll basic pullover.

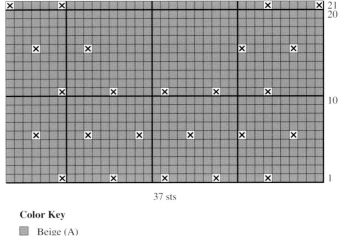

falling snow chart for pullover

37 sts

Color Key

- ▨ Beige (A)
- ☒ Ecru (C)

SLEEVES

Cast on and work rib with B. Change to larger needles.

Beg snow chart for sleeves

Row 1 (RS) Work 6 sts of snow chart 5 (5, 6) times, work first 4 (4, 0) sts once more. Cont as established until 4 rows of chart have been worked. Work in St st and stripe pat, complete foll basic pullover.

FINISHING

Complete foll basic pullover. Work neckband with A.

For nose, attach buttons as indicated on chart.

HAT

Using basic hat (page 13), cast on and work rib with A.

Change to larger needles. Work in St st for 1 row.

Beg snow chart

Row 1 (RS) Beg with row 2 (as a RS row) and work 6 sts of snow chart 12 (14) times, work first 5 (0) sts again. Cont as established until 3 rows of chart have been worked.

Beg reindeer chart

Row 1 (RS) Work 6 (4) sts A, *work 10 sts of reindeer chart, work 8 (10) sts A; rep from *, end last rep 7 (10) sts A. At the same time, complete foll basic hat. When chart is complete work 6 rows A, work with B to end. Cont as established until 15 rows of chart have been worked. Cont in St st and complete foll basic hat as foll: 6 rows A, then B to end.

EMBELLISHMENTS

Complete as for reindeer pullover.

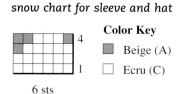

snow chart for sleeve and hat

Color Key
- ◼ Beige (A)
- ☐ Ecru (C)

6 sts

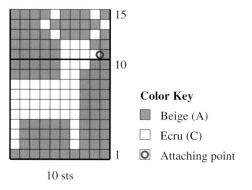

reindeer chart for hat

Color Key
- ◼ Beige (A)
- ☐ Ecru (C)
- ◉ Attaching point

10 sts

feeling sheepish

Materials

*Tahki Yarns/Tahki • Stacy Charles, Inc., Cotton Classic II,
1¾oz/50g skeins, each approx 74yd/68m (cotton)*

- *5 skeins in #2006 silver grey (A)*
- *3 skeins in #2001 white (C)*
- *1 skein in #2039 charcoal (B)*
- *One pair each sizes 5 and 7 (3.75 and 4.5mm)
  needles OR SIZE TO OBTAIN GAUGE*
- *Crochet hook size G/6 (4mm)*
- *Tapestry needle*
- *Four ½"/13mm white ball shank buttons*

Sample is shown in size 18 months.

Skill level

Intermediate

CARDIGAN

STRIPE PATTERN

*2 rows A, 2 rows C; rep from * (4 rows) for stripe pat.

BACK

Using basic cardigan (page 11), cast on and work rib with C. Change to larger
needles. Work in St st and stripe pat for 10 rows.

Beg lamb chart

Row 1 (RS) Work 5 (6, 7) sts A, *work 10 sts of lamb chart, work 6 sts A; rep
from *, end last rep 5 (6, 7) sts A. Cont as established until 10 rows of chart
have been worked. Cont with A only and complete foll basic cardigan.

lamb chart for cardigan and hat

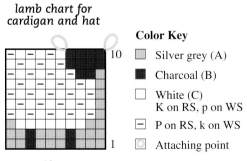

Color Key

- Silver grey (A)
- Charcoal (B)
- White (C)
  K on RS, p on WS
- − P on RS, k on WS
- Attaching point

10 sts

RIGHT FRONT

Work as for back through stripe pat.

Beg lamb chart

Row 1 (RS) Work 7 sts A, work 10 sts of lamb chart, work 7 (8, 9) sts A. Cont as established until 10 rows of chart have been worked. Cont with A only and complete foll basic cardigan.

LEFT FRONT

Work as for right front, reversing direction and placement of chart and all shaping.

SLEEVES

Cast on and work rib with C. Change to larger needles. Work in St st and stripe pat and complete foll basic cardigan.

FINISHING

Complete foll basic cardigan. Work bands with C, working buttonhole band on left front and button band on right front.

Sew buttons opposite buttonholes.

EMBELLISHMENTS

For ears (make 2), with crochet hook and B, ch 5, fasten off. Fold in half and sew center. Attach one side as indicated on chart.

HAT

Using basic hat (page 13), cast on and work rib with C. Change to larger needles. Work in St st and stripe pat for 4 rows.

Beg lamb chart for hat

Row 1 (RS) Work 6 (4) sts A, *work 10 sts of lamb chart, work 8 (10) sts A; rep from *, end last rep 7 (10) sts A. Cont as established until 10 rows of chart have been worked Cont in St st with A only and complete foll basic hat.

EMBELLISHMENTS

Work as for lamb cardigan.

MITTENS

Using basic mittens (page 14), cast on and work rib with C. Change to larger needles. Work in St st and stripe pat and complete foll basic mittens.

feeling sheepish

❖ ❖ ❖

Materials

Tahki Yarns/Tahki • Stacy Charles, Inc., Cotton Classic II, 1¾oz/50g skeins, each approx 74yd/68m (cotton)

- *8 skeins in #2001 white (C)*
- *6 skeins in #2006 silver grey (A)*
- *1 skein in #2039 charcoal (B)*
- *Size 7 (4.5mm) circular needle, 32"/80cm long OR SIZE TO OBTAIN GAUGE*
- *Crochet hook size G/6 (4mm)*

Blanket measures approx 28" x 34"/71cm x 86cm.

Skill level

Intermediate

STRIPE PATTERN

*2 rows A, 2 rows C; rep from * (4 rows) for stripe pat.

Note

4-st garter borders extend lengthwise on each side.

BLANKET

With C, cast on 124 sts. Work in garter st for 1"/2.5cm. Work 4 sts in garter st with C, work in St st and stripe pat to last 4 sts, work 4 sts in garter st with C. Cont as established until piece measures 25½"/65cm from beg, end with 2 rows C. Work in St st with A for 6 rows.

Beg lamb chart

Row 1 (RS) Cont 4 sts in garter st with C, work 19 sts A, *work 14 sts lamb chart, work 18 sts A; rep from * end last rep 19 sts A, cont last 4 sts in garter st with C. Cont as established until 18 rows of chart have been worked. Work in St st with A for 6 rows. Then work in St st, beg with C, stripe work in pat for 3"/7.5cm more, end with 2 rows A. With C, work in garter st for 1"/2.5cm. Bind off.

For eyes, use A and form French knots as indicated on chart.

For ears, with B, ch 8, fasten off. Sew center tog and attach one side as indicated on chart.

lamb chart for blanket

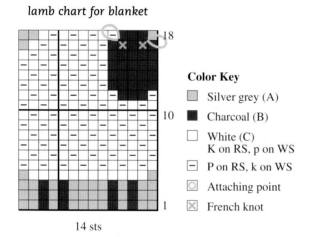

14 sts

Color Key

▦	Silver grey (A)
■	Charcoal (B)
☐	White (C) K on RS, p on WS
⊟	P on RS, k on WS
◎	Attaching point
☒	French knot

feeling sheepish

❖ ❖ ❖

Materials

Tahki Yarns/Tahki • Stacy Charles, Inc., Cotton Classic II, 1¾oz/50g skeins, each approx 74yd/68m (cotton)

- *3 skeins in #2006 silver grey (A)*
- *1 skein each in #2039 charcoal (B) and #2001 white (C)*
- *One pair each sizes 5 and 7 (3.75 and 4.5mm) needles OR SIZE TO OBTAIN GAUGE*
- *Crochet hook size G/6 (4mm)*
- *Three ½"/13mm white dome shank buttons*
- *10"/25.5cm square pillow form by Airtex*

Skill level

Intermediate

PILLOW

Using basic pillow (page 14), cast on with A. Foll basic pillow through first turning ridge. Cont with A and St st for 11 rows more.

Beg lamb pillow chart

Row 1 (RS) Work 10 sts A, work 26 sts of lamb pillow chart, work 10 sts A.

Cont as established until 36 rows of chart have been worked. Cont in St st with A only and work 11 rows more. Complete foll basic pillow.

FINISHING

Sew buttons opposite buttonholes.

For eyes, use A and form French knots as indicated on chart.

For ears, with B, ch 12, fasten off. Sew center tog and attach one side as indicated on chart.

lamb chart for pillow

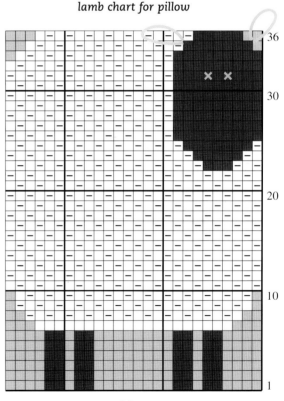

26 sts

Color Key

▧	Silver grey (A)
■	Charcoal (B)
☐	White (C) — K on RS, p on WS
⊟	P on RS, k on WS
☐	Attaching point
⊠	French knot

in the deep

❖ ❖ ❖

Deep rich colors teamed with

light-hearted motifs create

a balanced equation.

it takes two • in the navy • duck walk • sail away

He won't miss a fashion beat in a dashing

cardigan-and-cap set which combines stripes,

checks and a terrier motif for a look that shouts

"Great Scots"! Red alert—a winsome sheep

motif accented with novelty lamb buttons adds

flair to the striking ensemble below.

it takes two

✦✦✦

in the navy

✦✦✦

A perfect way to start off your fall knitting, this
sophisticated combo offers a fetching giraffe
pullover, matching hat and a comely afghan
perfectly suited for the nursery.

If she's off for a jaunt to the playground, be sure to outfit her in this toddler-chic duck pullover. If weather's brisk, compliment it with a matching hat and a pair of mitts to fight off nasty chills!

duck walk

❖ ❖ ❖

sail away

This dashing sailboat pullover takes you from
ship to shore in comfort and style. When the
sun falls and slumber sets, the afghan and
pillow do your little sailor justice.

it takes two

❖ ❖ ❖

Materials

Tahki Yarns/Tahki • Stacy Charles, Inc., Cotton Classic II,
1¾oz/50g skeins, each approx 74yd/68m (cotton)

- *5 skeins in #2744 green (B)*
- *2 skeins in #2861 navy (A)*
- *1 skein each in #2488 red (C) and*
  #2003 ecru (D)
- *One pair each sizes 5 and 7 (3.75 and 4.5mm)*
  needles OR SIZE TO OBTAIN GAUGE
- *Tapestry needle*
- *Six ⅝"/15mm red dog bone buttons for sweater*
- *Four ⅝"/15mm red dog bone buttons for hat*

Sample is shown in size 12 months.

Skill level

Intermediate

CARDIGAN

STRIPE PATTERN

*4 rows B, 4 rows A; rep from * (8 rows) for stripe pat.

BACK

Using basic cardigan (page 11), cast on and work rib with A. Change to larger needles.

Beg check chart

check chart

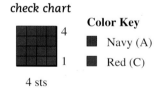

4

1

4 sts

Color Key

■ Navy (A)

■ Red (C)

Row 1 (RS) Work 4 sts of check chart 13 (13, 14) times, work first 0 (2, 0) sts once more. Cont as established until 4 rows of chart have been worked, then work rows 1 and 2 once more. Cont in St st with B only and complete foll basic cardigan.

RIGHT FRONT

Cast on and work rib with A. Change to larger needles.

Beg check chart

Row 1 (RS) Work 4 sts of check chart 6 times, work first 0 (1, 2) sts again. Cont as established until 6 rows of chart have been worked.

dog chart

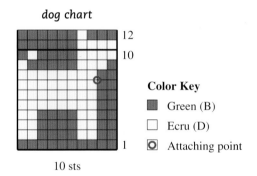

Color Key
- ■ Green (B)
- □ Ecru (D)
- ◉ Attaching point

10 sts

Beg dog chart

Row 1 (RS) Work 7 sts B, work 10 sts of dog chart, work 7 (8, 9) sts B. Cont as established until 12 rows of chart have been worked. Cont in St st and B only and complete foll basic cardigan.

LEFT FRONT

Work as for right front, reversing direction and placement of chart and all shaping.

SLEEVES

Cast on and work rib with A. Change to larger needles.

Beg check chart

Row 1 (RS) Work 4 sts of check chart 8 (8, 9) times, work first 2 (2, 0) sts once more. Cont as established until 4 rows of chart have been worked. Working in St st and stripe pat, complete foll basic cardigan.

FINISHING

Complete foll basic cardigan. Work bands with B, working buttonhole band on left front and button band on right front.

Sew buttons opposite buttonholes.

EMBELLISHMENTS

Sew buttons on dog as indicated on chart.

it takes two

❖ ❖ ❖

Materials

Tahki Yarns/Tahki • Stacy Charles, Inc., Cotton Classic II,
1¾oz/50g skeins, each approx 74yd/68m (cotton)

- *5 skeins in #2744 green (B)*
- *2 skeins in #2861 navy (A)*
- *1 skein each in #2488 red (C) and*
  #2003 ecru (D)
- *One pair each sizes 5 and 7 (3.75 and 4.5mm)*
  needles OR SIZE TO OBTAIN GAUGE
- *Tapestry needle*
- *Six ⅝"/15mm red dog bone buttons for sweater*
- *Four ⅝"/15mm red dog bone buttons for hat*

Skill level

Intermediate

HAT

Using basic hat (page 13), cast on and work rib with A. Change to larger needles.

Beg check chart

Row 1 (RS) Work 4 sts of check chart 19 (21) times, work first 1 (0) st once more. Cont as established until 4 rows of chart have been worked.

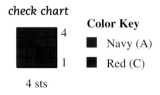

check chart

4

1

4 sts

Color Key

■ Navy (A)

■ Red (C)

Beg dog chart

Row 1 (RS) Work 8 sts A, *work 10 sts of dog chart, work 7(9) sts A; rep from *, end last rep 8 (9) sts A. Cont as established until 12 rows of chart have been worked. Cont in St st and complete foll basic hat as foll: 6 rows B, then work in C to end.

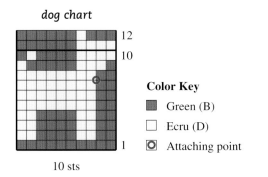

dog chart

10 sts

Color Key
- ■ Green (B)
- □ Ecru (D)
- ⊙ Attaching point

FINISHING

Sew buttons on dog as indicated on chart.

MITTENS

Using basic mitten (page 14), cast on and work rib with A. Change to larger needles. Cont in St st and stripe pat and complete foll basic mittens.

it takes two

❖ ❖ ❖

Materials

Tahki Yarns/Tahki • Stacy Charles, Inc., Cotton Classic II,
1¾oz/50g skeins, each approx 74yd/68m (cotton)

- *5 skeins in #2488 red (B)*
- *1 skein each in #2861 navy (A), #2003 ecru (D)*
- *Small amount of #2744 green (C)*
- *One pair each sizes 5 and 7 (3.75 and 4.5mm)*
  needles OR SIZE TO OBTAIN GAUGE
- *Crochet hook size G/6 (4mm)*
- *Tapestry needle*
- *Four ½"/13mm blue lamb buttons*

Sample is shown in size 6 months.

Skill level

Intermediate

CARDIGAN

BACK

Using basic cardigan (page 11), cast on and work rib with B. Change to larger needles. Cont in St st with B only and complete foll basic cardigan.

RIGHT FRONT

Cast on and work rib with B. Change to larger needles. Work in St st for 4 rows.

Beg lamb chart

Row 1 (RS) Work 5 sts B, work 14 st of lamb chart, work 5 (6, 7) sts B.

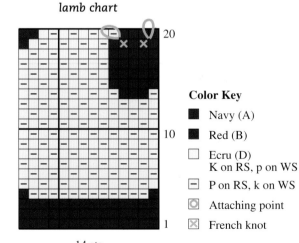

lamb chart

20

10

1

14 sts

Color Key

- ■ Navy (A)
- ■ Red (B)
- □ Ecru (D)
  K on RS, p on WS
- − P on RS, k on WS
- ⊙ Attaching point
- ⊠ French knot

Cont as established until 20 rows of chart have been worked. Cont with B only and complete foll basic cardigan.

LEFT FRONT

Work as for right front, reversing direction and placement of chart and all shaping.

SLEEVES

Cast on and work rib with B. Change to larger needles. Working in St st with B only, complete foll basic cardigan.

FINISHING

Complete foll basic cardigan. Work bands with B, working buttonhole band on left front and button band on right front.

Sew buttons opposite buttonholes.

EMBELLISHMENTS

For eyes use one strand of C and form French knot as indicated on chart.

For ears (make 2), with crochet hook and A, ch 8, fasten off. Fold in half and sew center. Attach one side as indicated on chart.

HAT

Using basic hat (page 13), cast on and work rib with B.

Change to larger needles. Work in St st for 2 rows.

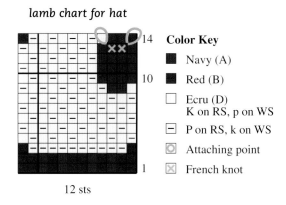

lamb chart for hat

Color Key
- ■ Navy (A)
- ■ Red (B)
- □ Ecru (D) K on RS, p on WS
- ⊟ P on RS, k on WS
- ◎ Attaching point
- ☒ French knot

12 sts

Beg lamb chart for hat

Row 1 (RS) Work 32 (36) sts B, work 12 sts of lamb chart, work 33 (36) sts B. Cont as established until 14 rows of chart have been worked. Cont in St st with B only and complete foll basic hat.

EMBELLISHMENTS

For eyes, work as for lamb cardigan

For ears (make 2), with crochet hook and A, ch 6, fasten off. Fold in half and sew center. Attach one side as indicated on chart.

in the navy

❖ ❖ ❖

PULLOVER

STRIPE PATTERN

*4 rows B, 4 rows A; rep from * (8 rows) for stripe pat.

BACK

Using basic pullover (page 12), cast on and work rib with A. Change to larger needles. Cont in St st with A only and complete foll basic pullover.

FRONT

Cast on and work rib with A. Change to larger needles. Work in St st for 14 rows.

Beg giraffe chart

Row 1 (RS) Work 15 (16, 17) sts A, work 22 sts of giraffe chart, work 15 (16, 17) sts A. Cont as established until 30 rows of chart have been worked. Cont in St st with A only and complete foll basic pullover.

giraffe chart

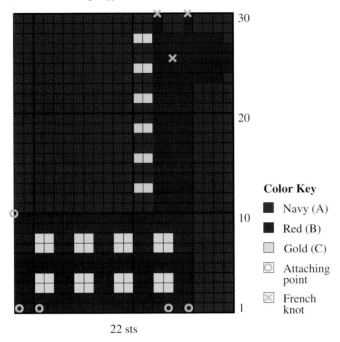

30

20

Color Key

◼ Navy (A)
◼ Red (B)
◻ Gold (C)
⊙ Attaching point
⊠ French knot

10

1

22 sts

SLEEVES

Cast on and work rib with A. Change to larger needles.

Working in St st and stripe pat, complete foll basic pullover.

FINISHING

Complete foll basic pullover. Work neckband with A.

EMBELLISHMENTS

For eyes, use one strand of A and form French knot as indicated on chart.

For tail, with crochet hook and B, chain 1½"/4cm. Fasten off and attach as indicated on chart.

For horn (knobs), with 2 strands of B, form French knot as indicated on chart.

For legs (make 2), with larger needles and C, cast on 7 sts. Work in garter st for 3 rows. Join B and work in St st for 13 rows. Bind off.

With WS tog, sew side and lower edges. Attach as indicated on chart, hang loose.

HAT

Using basic hat (page 13), cast on and work rib with A. Change to larger needles. Work in St st and stripe pat and complete foll basic hat.

in the navy

❖ ❖ ❖

Materials

Tahki Yarns/Tahki • Stacy Charles, Inc., Cotton Classic II,
1¾oz/50g skeins, each approx 74yd/68m (cotton)

- *6 skeins in #2861 navy (A)*
- *4 skeins in #2488 red (B)*
- *3 skeins in #2744 green (E)*
- *1 skein in #2567 gold (C) and #2003 ecru (D)*
- *Size 7 (4.5mm) circular needle, 32"/80cm long*
  OR SIZE TO OBTAIN GAUGE
- *Crochet hook size G/6 (4mm)*
- *Silver bell on shank ½"/13mm (may also be*
  embroidered using silver embroidery thread)

Afghan measures approx 28" x 38"/71cm x 96.5cm.

Skill level

Intermediate

Notes

1 Work blocks in St st (unless otherwise indicated) with separate balls of yarn for each block. Twist yarns on WS to prevent holes.

2 4-st garter borders extend lengthwise on each side.

3 Each block is 29 sts x 36 rows.

AFGHAN

With A, cast on 124 sts. Work in garter st for 1"/2.5cm.

Row 1 (RS) Cont 4 sts in garter st with A, work blocks foll diagram for placement, cont last 4 sts in garter st with A. Cont as established until all blocks have been worked. With A, work in garter st for 1"/2.5cm. Bind off.

SOLID BLOCK

Work on 29 sts and 36 rows using A, B or E.

CHART BLOCKS

Work 29 sts and 36 rows as foll:

GIRAFFE

Rows 1 to 12 St st with A.

Rows 13 to 33 Work 21 rows of giraffe chart as foll: 7 sts A,

15 sts giraffe chart, 7 sts A.

Rows 34 to 36 St st with A.

giraffe chart

Color Key

- ■ Navy (A)
- ■ Red (B)
- □ Gold (C)
- ◎ Attaching point
- ☒ French knot

15 sts

LAMB

Rows 1 to 8 St st with B.

Rows 9 to 28 Work 20 rows of lamb chart as foll: 8 sts B, 14

sts lamb chart, 7 sts B.

Rows 29 to 36 St st with B.

lamb chart

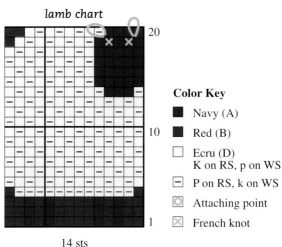

Color Key

- ■ Navy (A)
- ■ Red (B)
- □ Ecru (D)
  K on RS, p on WS
- – P on RS, k on WS
- ◎ Attaching point
- ☒ French knot

14 sts

DUCK

Rows 1 to 6 St st with A.

Rows 7 to 31 Work 25 rows of duck chart as foll: 6 sts A, 16

sts duck chart, 7 sts A.

Rows 32 to 36 St st with A.

duck chart

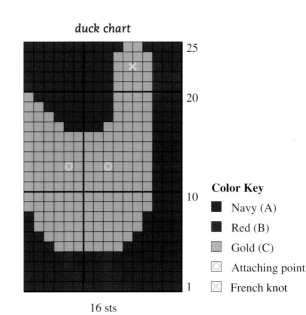

Color Key

- ■ Navy (A)
- ■ Red (B)
- ■ Gold (C)
- ◎ Attaching point
- ☒ French knot

16 sts

EMBELLISHMENTS

Giraffe

See instructions for embellishing giraffe pullover, making tail 1"/2.5cm long.

For legs (make 2), with larger needles and C, cast on 5 sts. Work in garter st for 3 rows. Join B and work in St st for 9 rows. Complete as giraffe pullover.

Lamb

See instructions for embellishing lamb cardigan. (see page 105).

Duck

For eye, use one strand of E and form French knot as indicated on chart.

For wing, with C, cast on 6 sts. Work in St st for 4 rows. Dec 1 st each side every other row twice. Cut yarn and draw through rem sts, fasten off tightly. Attach as indicated on chart.

diagram for multi-patch blanket

duck walk

❖ ❖ ❖

Materials

Tahki Yarns/Tahki • Stacy Charles, Inc., Cotton Classic II, 1¾oz/50g skeins, each approx 74yd/68m (cotton)

- *6 skeins (plus 1 skein for each hat) in #2801 teal (A)*
- *1 skein each in #2488 red (B), #2003 ecru (C), #2567 gold (D) and #2924 purple (E)*
- *One pair each sizes 5 and 7 (3.75 and 4.5mm) needles OR SIZE TO OBTAIN GAUGE*
- *Crochet hook size G/6 (4mm)*
- *Tapestry needle*
- *Piece of red felt*

Sample is shown in size 18 months.

Skill level

Intermediate

PULLOVER

BACK

Using basic pullover (page 12), cast on and work rib with A. Change to larger needles.

fence chart

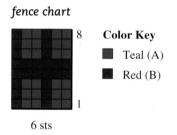

8

1

6 sts

Color Key

◼ Teal (A)

◼ Red (B)

Beg fence chart

Row 1 (RS) Work 6 sts fence chart 8 (9, 9) times, work first 4 (0, 2) sts once more. Cont as established until 8 rows of chart have been worked. Work in St st and A only and complete foll basic pullover.

FRONT

Work as for back until fence chart complete. Work in St st for 20 rows with A.

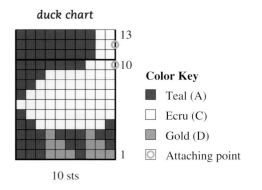

duck chart

13
10
1

Color Key
- ■ Teal (A)
- □ Ecru (C)
- ▨ Gold (D)
- ◎ Attaching point

10 sts

Beg duck chart

Row 1 (RS) Work 6 (7, 8) sts A, *work 10 sts of duck chart, work 5 sts A; rep from *, end last rep 6 (7, 8) sts A. Cont as established until 13 rows of chart have been worked. Work in St st and A only and complete foll basic pullover.

RIGHT SLEEVE

Cast on and work rib with A. Change to larger needles. Work in St st for 4 rows.

Beg duck chart

Row 1 (RS) Work 6 sts A, work 10 sts of duck chart, work 18 (18, 20) sts A. Cont as established until 13 rows of chart have been worked. Work in St st and A only and complete foll basic pullover.

LEFT SLEEVE

Work as for right sleeve, reversing direction and placement of duck chart as foll: work 18 (18, 20) sts A, work 10 sts of duck chart, work 6 sts A.

FINISHING

Complete foll basic pullover. Work neckband with A.

EMBELLISHMENTS

For scarf, with crochet hook and B, chain 1½"/4cm. Fasten off and attach as indicated on chart by looping around duck's neck. Leave ends loose and knot.

For beaks, with crochet hook and D, ch 7, fasten off. Fold in half and sew center. Attach one side as indicated on chart.

duck walk

❖ ❖ ❖

Materials

Tahki Yarns/Tahki • Stacy Charles, Inc., Cotton Classic II,

1¾oz/50g skeins, each approx 74yd/68m (cotton)

- *6 skeins (plus 1 skein for each hat) in #2801 teal (A)*
- *1 skein each in #2488 red (B), #2003 ecru (C), #2567 gold (D) and #2924 purple (E)*
- *One pair each sizes 5 and 7 (3.75 and 4.5mm) needles OR SIZE TO OBTAIN GAUGE*
- *Crochet hook size G/6 (4mm)*
- *Tapestry needle*
- *Piece of red felt*

Skill level

Intermediate

DUCK HAT

Using basic hat (page 13), cast on and work rib with A. Change to larger needles. Work in St st for 2 rows.

Beg duck chart

Row 1 (RS) Work 6 (8) sts A, *work 10 sts of duck chart, work 8 (9) sts A; rep from *, end last rep 7 (9) sts A. Cont as established until 13 rows of chart have been worked. Cont in St st and complete foll basic hat as foll: 7 rows A, then work in C to end.

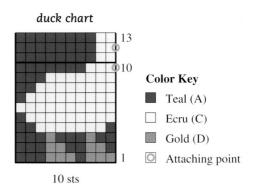

duck chart

13

⓪ 10

Color Key

■ Teal (A)
□ Ecru (C)
▨ Gold (D)
⊚ Attaching point

1

10 sts

EMBELLISHMENTS

Complete as for duck pullover.

PATCH HAT

Using basic hat (page 13), cast on and work rib with A. Change to larger needles. Work 39 (42) sts E, work 38 (42) sts B. Cont as established for 1 row more.

patch chart

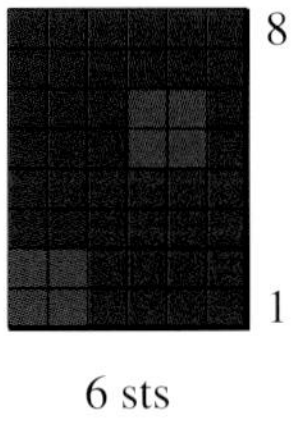

6 sts

Color Key
- ■ Red (B)
- ■ Purple (E)

Beg duck and patch chart.

Row 1 (RS) Work 25 (27) sts E, work 10 sts of duck chart, work 4 (5) sts E, then work 6 (7) sts of patch chart 6 times, work first 2 (0) sts once more. Cont as established until 13 rows of duck chart and 3 rows E, and 16 rows of patch chart have been worked, then work in St st and complete foll basic hat as foll: [2 rows A, 2 rows E] twice, then B to end.

EMBELLISHMENTS

Complete as for duck pullover.

MITTENS

Using basic mitten (page 14), cast on and work rib with A. Change to larger needles. Cont in St st until piece measures 4"/10cm from beg. With B, complete foll basic mittens.

sail away

❖ ❖ ❖

Materials

*Tahki Yarns/Tahki • Stacy Charles, Inc., Cotton Classic II,
1¾oz/50g skeins, each approx 74yd/68m (cotton)*

- *6 skeins in #2861 navy (A)*
- *1 skein each in #2533 yellow (B), #2997 red (C)
  and #2001 white (D)*
- *One pair each sizes 5 and 7 (3.75 and 4.5mm)
  needles OR SIZE TO OBTAIN GAUGE*
- *Crochet hook size G/6 (4mm)*
- *Tapestry needle*
- *Piece of red felt*

Sample is shown in size 12 months.

Skill level

Intermediate

BACK

Using basic pullover (page 12), cast on and work rib with A. Change to larger
needles. Work in St st with D for 4 rows.

Beg wave chart

Row 1 (RS) Work 6 sts wave chart 8 (9, 9) times, work first 4 (0, 2) sts once
more. Cont as established until 2 rows of chart have been worked. Work in St
st and A only and complete foll basic pullover.

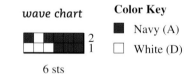

wave chart   **Color Key**

■ Navy (A)

□ White (D)

6 sts

FRONT

Work as for back until wave chart is complete. Work in St st for 4 rows with A.

Beg sail boat chart

Row 1 (RS) Work 2 (3, 4) sts A, *work 13 sts of sail boat chart, work 4 sts A; rep from *, end last rep 3 (4, 5) sts A. Cont as established until 10 rows of chart have been worked. Work in St st and A only and complete foll basic pullover.

sail boat chart for pullover

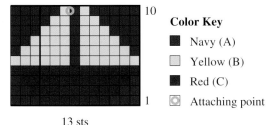

13 sts

Color Key

■ Navy (A)

□ Yellow (B)

■ Red (C)

◉ Attaching point

SLEEVES

Cast on and work rib with A. Change to larger needles. Work in St st with D for 2 rows.

Beg wave chart

Row 1 (RS) Work 6 sts wave chart 5 (5, 6) times, work first 4 (4, 0) sts once more. Cont as established until 2 rows of chart have been worked. Work in St st and A only and complete foll basic pullover.

FINISHING

Complete foll basic pullover. Work neckband with A.

EMBELLISHMENTS

Using flag template, cut out 3 flags from felt. Attach as indicated on chart.

HAT

Using basic hat (page 13), cast on and work rib with A. Change to larger needles. Work in St st with D for 2 rows.

Beg wave chart

Row 1 (RS) Work 6 sts wave chart 12 (14) times, work first 5 (0) sts once more. Cont as established until 2 rows of chart have been worked. Work in St st with A for 2 rows.

Beg sail boat chart

Row 1 (RS) Work 6 (4) sts A, *work 11 sts of sail boat chart, work 7 (9) sts A; rep from *, end last rep 6 (9) sts A. Cont as established until 8 rows of chart have been worked.

Work in St st complete foll basic hat as foll: 8 rows A, 2 rows D, 2 rows A, 2 rows D, then A only to end of piece.

sail boat chart for hat

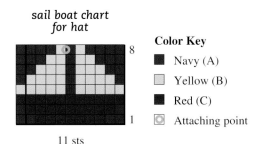

11 sts

Color Key

■ Navy (A)

□ Yellow (B)

■ Red (C)

◉ Attaching point

FINISHING

Complete as for sail boat pullover.

Felt pattern

sail away

❖ ❖ ❖

Materials

Tahki Yarns/Tahki • Stacy Charles, Inc., Cotton Classic II,
1¾oz/50g skeins, each approx 74yd/68m (cotton)

- *5 skeins in #2861 navy (A)*
- *4 skeins each in #2533 yellow (B) and*
  #2997 red (C)
- *Size 7 (4.5mm) circular needle, 32"/80cm long*

Afghan measures approx 28" x 38"/71cm x 96.5cm.

Skill level

Intermediate

Notes

1 Work blocks in St st with separate balls of yarn for each block. Twist yarns on WS to prevent holes.

2 4-st garter borders extend lengthwise on each side.

3 Each block is 29 sts x 36 rows.

AFGHAN

With A, cast on 124 sts. Work in garter st for 1"/2.5cm.

Row 1 (RS) Cont 4 sts in garter st with A, work blocks in St st, foll diagram for placement, cont last 4 sts in garter st with A. Cont as established until all blocks have been worked. With A, work in garter st for 1"/2.5cm. Bind off.

SOLID BLOCK

Work 29 sts and 36 rows using A, B or C.

SAILBOAT BLOCK

Work 29 sts and 36 row as foll:

Rows 1 to 8 St st with A.

Rows 9 to 28 Work 20 rows of sailboat chart as foll: 6 sts A, 17 sts sailboat chart, 6 sts A.

Rows 29 to 36 St st with A.

FINISHING

For sails, with C, cast on 4 sts. Work in St st for 2 rows. Dec 1 st each side on next row. P 1 row. Cut yarn and pull through rem sts and fasten off tightly. Attach edge of sail as indicated on chart.

sail boat chart

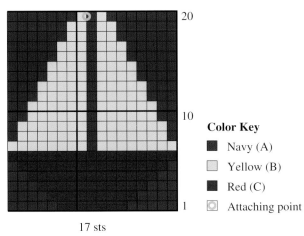

Color Key

■ Navy (A)
□ Yellow (B)
■ Red (C)
◎ Attaching point

sail away

Materials

Tahki Yarns/Tahki • Stacy Charles, Inc., Cotton Classic II,
1¾oz/50g skeins, each approx 74yd/68m (cotton)

- *3 skeins in #2861 navy (A)*
- *1 skein each in #2533 yellow (B) and #2997 red (C)*
- *One pair each sizes 5 and 7 (3.75 and 4.5mm) needles OR SIZE TO OBTAIN GAUGE*
- *Three ½"/13mm red shank buttons*
- *10"/25.5cm square pillow form*

Skill level

Intermediate

PILLOW

Using basic pillow (page 14), cast on with A. Foll basic pillow through first turning ridge. Work in St st with A for 11 rows more.

Beg sailboat pillow chart

Row 1 (RS) Work 9 sts A, work 29 sts of sailboat pillow chart, work 8 sts A. Cont as established until 36 rows of chart have been worked. Cont in St st with A only and work 11 rows more. Complete foll basic pillow.

sailboat pillow chart

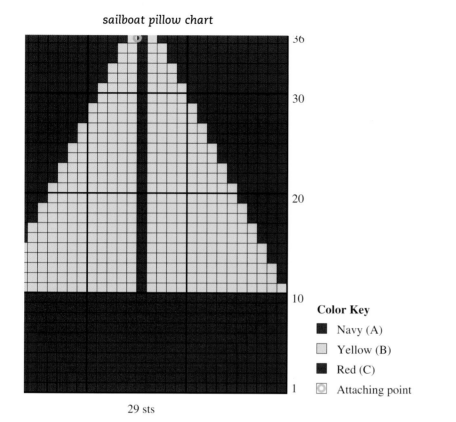

36
30
20
10
1

29 sts

Flag template

Color Key

■ Navy (A)
□ Yellow (B)
■ Red (C)
◉ Attaching point

FINISHING

Sew buttons opposite buttonholes.

For sail, With C, cast on 6 sts. Work in St st for 4 rows.

Dec 1 st each side every other row twice. Cut yarn and

draw through rem sts, fasten off tightly. Attach as indicated

on chart.

acknowledgments

❖ ❖ ❖

This book took on a special meaning to me, thanks to the people who helped along the way. Special thanks to my mother and late father, who always supported my dreams and taught me to give my heart to whatever I chose to do. Thank you to my sister, who gave me three hours of extra ear time from the west coast during overwhelming moments of "knitomania." Also, thank you to my two soccer-crazed nephews, who were my first muses, and continue to be reservoirs of inspiration. I give eternal gratitude to Janet, who responded patiently to all my questions, such as "Which green do you like better?" To Margaret, I thank you for all of your practical insight, and much appreciated encouragement. Thank you to Ed, a true dear friend, who did not flinch no matter how many opinions I asked of him. Also, a special thanks to Ruth Scharf—my former boss and an excellent teacher, who raised my standard of work ethic, color and design. Thank you to the staff at Sixth&Spring Books: Michelle Lo, Shannon Kerner, Veronica Manno, Carla Scott, Charlotte Parry, Chi Ling Moy, Mary Helt and Dan Howell. I owe a special thanks to Trisha Malcolm, who has been such an encouraging friend for so many years. She made this dream come true. Finally, a special thanks goes to all the fine creatures of the animal kingdom that inspire me daily; thanks for being such good sports about all this!

resources

❖ ❖ ❖

Blue Moon Buttons Art

25 Clover Drive

Bayfield, CO 81122

www.bluemoonbuttons.com

Brown Sheep Co.

100662 County Road 16

Mitchell, NE 69357

www.brownsheep.com

Tahki Yarns

distributed by

Tahki • Stacy Charles, Inc.

Tahki • Stacy Charles, Inc.

70-30 80th Street

Building 36

Ridgewood, NY 11385

www.tahkistacycharles.com

We have made every effort to ensure the accuracy of the contents
of this publication. We are not responsible for any
human or typographic errors.